The Right to Picket and
the Freedom of Public Discourse

JOHN W. WHITEHEAD

The Right to Picket and the Freedom of Public Discourse

THE RUTHERFORD INSTITUTE REPORT: VOLUME 3

Crossway Books   Westchester, Illinois
A Division of Good News Publishers

The Right to Picket and the Freedom of Public Discourse. Copyright ©
1984 by the Rutherford Institute. Published by Crossway Books, a
division of Good News Publishers, Westchester, Illinois 60153.

The Rutherford Institute Report: Volume 3

First printing, 1984

Printed in the United States of America

Library of Congress Catalog Card Number 84-72425

ISBN 0-89107-344-2

Note: This book is not intended to be, and does not constitute, the
giving of legal advice. Particular court decisions may not apply to
particular factual situations, or may not be legally binding in
particular jurisdictions. The existence of many unfavorable
decisions indicates that reliance should not be placed on the
favorable decisions as necessarily dispositive or assuring victory.
This book is not intended to substitute for individual reliance on
privately retained legal counsel.

Contents

Acknowledgments

There are many people involved in any project. Such is the case with this book.

David Melton, my legal intern, provided a steady flow of good research to me. His many hours of work are appreciated. Moreover, Clarence Pollard's work on some of the final details of this book was helpful.

March Bell, executive director of the Rutherford Institute, and Rebecca Beane, my administrative assistant, were very supportive during the many hours of putting this book together. I am also very thankful to my wife, Carol, and my five children for their continued support.

Franky Schaeffer's insight and creativity were a great help, as were the advice and wise counsel of Jim Buchfuehrer and Tom Neuberger.

I would like to thank Crossway Books, especially Lane and Jan Dennis, for their continued assistance with the *Rutherford Reports*. Ted Griffin's editorial assistance is also appreciated.

Finally, I express my gratitude to the countless individuals across this country who are willing to stand for truth. Without you, the flame of freedom would not burn as brightly.

John W. Whitehead

Foreword

Many prolife activists, such as myself, believe the time has long passed when we could in good conscience sit on our hands and allow society to take its course concerning abortion and a host of other related issues. In opposing the manifold evils of the day, Christian activists and other prolifers will welcome this book by John Whitehead. Essentially a legal handbook, it clearly spells out for the layman (but with fully footnoted references for the legal scholar) the parameters of picketing, protest, and other forms of public discourse which prolifers and others concerned about the pressing moral issues of the day must now begin to use if they wish to change the course of history in this country.

We must be willing to risk liberty and, yes, even life in the cause of truth. However, there is no point in becoming a martyr, losing one's life, or for that matter even spending a night in jail if it is unnecessary. Here in this *Rutherford Report* are recommendations and legal principles which will help the Christian activist, the pro-life picketer, and the sidewalk counselor avoid pitfalls while still voicing his or her opinion in public through demonstrations and other means.

John Whitehead and the Rutherford Institute have become faithful servants of the prolife cause in defending picketers who have been arrested, pressing for the reinstatement of the legal rights of the unborn, and providing information such as that contained in this book. I would urge all who read this book, who are not already on the Rutherford mailing list, to write to the Rutherford Insitute, Box 510, Manassas, VA 22110, to begin receiving the *Rutherford Newsletter.* It will keep you posted on legal developments as they affect Christian activism, religious civil liberties, and the freedom of speech. With gratitude to John Whitehead for once again providing us with thoughtful and informative material, I urge you to carefully study this book, use the information to help you express your opinion, and use your constitutional rights as an American citizen to change this country for the better.

Franky Schaeffer

The Right to Picket and
the Freedom of Public Discourse

A popular government, without popular information, or the means of acquiring it, is but a Prologue to a Farce or a Tragedy; or, perhaps both. Knowledge will forever govern Ignorance: And a people who mean to be their own Governors, must arm themselves with the power which knowledge gives.

James Madison

Congress shall make no law respecting an establishment of religion, or prohibiting the free exercise thereof; or abridging the freedom of speech, or of the press; or the right of the people peaceably to assemble, and to petition the Government for a redress of grievances.

The First Amendment

Introduction

A function of free speech . . . is to invite dispute. It may indeed best serve its high purpose when it induces . . . unrest . . . or even stirs people to anger.

Justice William O. Douglas

Freedom for religious, social, and political self-expression is not an appendage to, but rather is at the heart of, our political system. Inherent in this right of self-expression is the possibility for peaceful change in our society. This ability to change the system through the system is a vital part of our form of government and national heritage.

Incorporated into this system are certain safeguards, commonly referred to as the Bill of Rights. These liberties are guarantees against *governmental* intrusion. Under the original federal Constitution, this schedule of immunities provided protection against the central government. The state governments were free to regulate as they would. Judicial interpretation of the Fourteenth Amendment has, since 1925, applied the Bill of Rights against the states. Thus, the state governments are now restricted by the federal Consitution's protections for individual liberty.

The First Amendment enumerates the dearest of these freedoms—the liberty of freely exercising one's

1

religion, of press, of speech, of assembly, and of petition for the redress of grievances. These rights, far from being the mere creation of judges and jurists, are God-given liberties. The First Amendment is not a matter of legislative grace, but a recognition of those inherent and inalienable rights necessary in the American compact between the government and the governed.

These civil liberties are not limitless. Legislative and judicial encroachments have encrusted these guarantees with doctrines and restrictions to the point that they are hardly recognizable.

Because of the growing responsiveness and awareness of various segments of the American community to social change, an understanding of basic free-expression liberties and their judicial interpretation is vital. Persons from various walks of life who previously would have never dreamed of participating in religious, social, and political activism are becoming involved. Social responsibility is being shouldered.

How Should We Then Conduct Ourselves?

In the United States, under the Constitution, the question is not "May I dissent?" or "May I oppose the actions of government or individuals?" To the contrary, I not only have the right to dissent, criticize, and oppose, but in some circumstances I also have a moral duty to do so. The Constitution guarantees this.

The crucial questions, therefore, are these: "How may I dissent?" and "How should I conduct myself when dissenting, opposing or criticizing?"

Each of us has a duty of obedience to the law. This is a moral as well as a legal imperative. Therefore, a first question must be: "What are the means of lawful expression?" This, of course, brings us to a related question: "What are the means of opposition and dissent that are permissible under our system of law and which therefore will not subject us to punishment by the state and will not violate our duty of obedience to the law?"

In discussing these important concerns, this book will focus on two related types of expressive conduct which, while in some respects controversial, are nonetheless vital freedoms: the right to public discourse and disputation, and the right to picket. However, this book is *not* intended to tell one *what "the law" ought to be.* Only individual conscience, sincerity, and, most important, the obedience to the Higher Law can prescribe where those boundaries are. However, this book is intended to tell one what "the law" currently is.*

The freedom to publicly speak one's mind and, if necessary, to publicly picket as a form of free expression has long been a part of our fundamental law. As Supreme Court Justice Abe Fortas has written:

> From our earliest history, we have insisted that each of us is and must be free to criticize the government, however sharply; to express dissent and opposition, however brashly; even to advocate overthrow of the government itself. We have insisted upon freedom of speech and of the press and, as the First Amendment to the Constitution puts it, upon "the right of the people peaceably to assemble and to petition the Government for a redress of grievances."[1]

Both *advocacy* and *action* are protected under the Constitution when carried forth peaceably. *Violence*, how-

---

*The constitutional position outlined in this book is believed to be accurate as a matter of correct constitutional interpretation, but is not universally accepted by courts. Courts often are not solicitous of constitutional rights, and this may be particularly so in cases dealing with issues addressed in this book. Therefore, one should not rely on the constitutional arguments given in this book as being accepted by all courts. Further, those who face actual or potential prosecution for expressive conduct should retain a qualified attorney with constitutional expertise. No reliance should be placed on this book as a substitute for individual legal counsel or for privately retained representation.

ever, *is not protected.* Physical attacks upon persons and destruction of property is without the law. Such should not be condoned and practiced by those seeking meaningful change in free governments. Instead, violence should be condemned (as should all unrestrained abuses), or an anarchy could result. As the United States Supreme Court has recognized:

> Civil liberties, as guaranteed by the Constitution, imply the existence of an organized society maintaining public order without which liberty itself would be lost in the excesses of unrestrained abuses.[2]

How should we then conduct ourselves? The answer should be obvious to those intent on preserving freedom: peaceably, nonviolently, and without malice toward our fellowman.

Part One

Constitutional Principles

[The First Amendment] extends to more than abstract discussion, unrelated to action. The First Amendment is a charter for government, not for an institution of learning. "Free trade in ideas" means free trade in the opportunity to persuade to action, not merely to describe facts.

Thomas v Collins, 323 U.S. 516, 537 (1945)

1

Truth in the Marketplace

Those who begin coercive elimination of dissent soon find themselves exterminating dissenters. Compulsory unification of opinion achieves only the unanimity of the graveyard.

> *West Virginia Board of Education v. Barnette,*
> 319 U.S. 624, 641 (1943)

Poet John Milton, in his classic 1644 tract *Areopagitica,* wrote: "[T]hough all winds of doctrine were let loose to play upon the earth, so truth be in the field, we do injuriously, by licensing, and prohibiting, to misdoubt her strength. Let her and falsehood grapple; whoever knew truth put to the worse in a free and open encounter?"[1]

The concept that ideas must compete in the marketplace of men's minds and hearts is the credo of First Amendment judicial theory. Press, speech, and other forms of expressive conduct are the mediums by which these ideas are distributed.

One early American proponent of this marketplace of ideas concept was United States Supreme Court Justice Oliver Wendell Holmes, Jr. In his dissenting opinion in the case of *Abrams v. United States,*[2] Holmes first introduced the concept to the Court.

The best articulated rationale for this theory was

provided by Justice Felix Frankfurter in *Kovacs v. Cooper*,[3] some thirty years later:

> [T]he progress of civilization is to a considerable extent the displacement of error which once held sway as official truth by beliefs which in turn have yielded to other beliefs. . . . [T]he right to search for truth [is] of a different order than some transient economic dogma. And without freedom of expression, thought becomes checked and atrophied. . . . [T]hose liberties of the individual which history has attested as the indispensable conditions of an open as against a closed society come to this Court with a momentum for respect lacking when appeal is made to liberties which derive merely from shifting economic arrangements.[4]

Within this marketplace the First Amendment grants a large area of protection. The United States Supreme Court has made it abundantly clear that "all ideas having even the slightest redeeming social importance—unorthodox ideas, controversial ideas, even ideas hateful to the prevailing climate of opinion—have the full protection of the [constitutional] guaranties."[5] The avoidance of censorship, the Supreme Court has stressed, is to "preserve an uninhibited marketplace of ideas in which truth will ultimately prevail."[6]

Because of the participatory nature of American government, the preservation of our society as a marketplace of ideas is vital for freedom. "[S]peech concerning public affairs," the Supreme Court has said, "is more than self-expression; it is the essence of self-government"[7] and, as such, "has always rested on the highest rung of the hierarchy of First Amendment values."[8] Thus, as the Court has held: "[T]here is a profound national commitment to the principle that 'debate on public issues should be uninhibited, robust, and wide open.' "[9]

The idea of an "open society" is the theoretical underpinning for the freedom of the press, speech, and the right to engage in expressive *conduct*. This is all the more important when discussing the right to address oneself to ideas in public (such as religious preaching on a street corner), or the right to peaceably picket in public in seeking a redress of grievances. These types of public discourse, although controversial and even distasteful to some, must be protected against interference if we are to preserve truth in the marketplace of society for all.

2

The Freedoms of Religion, Speech, Assembly, and Petition, and the Right to Receive Information

> The established elements of speech, assembly, association and petition, "though not identical, are inseparable."
> *NAACP v. Claiborne Hardware,*
> 458 U.S. 886, 911 (1982)

The constitutional rights of religion, speech and press, assembly and petition, whether by accident or design, seem to be enumerated in an order. All of these freedoms embody a reverence for the individual conscience and the expression of the conscience. This fact was addressed by the United States Supreme Court in a 1969 decision:

> The makers of our Constitution undertook to secure conditions favorable to the pursuit of happiness. They recognized the significance of man's spiritual nature, of his feelings and of his intellect. . . . They sought to protect Americans in their beliefs, their thoughts, their emotions and their sensations. They conferred, as against the Government, the right to be let alone.[1]

Because they emanate from the individual, these rights partake more and more of conduct and less and less of conscience as one progresses down the list of enumerated First Amendment rights. Since the amount of protection afforded will be determined by the nature of the expressive activity, all self-expression can be viewed as a continuum, with "pure speech" on one end and "pure conduct" on the other. Thus, in some instances pure conduct may not be constitutionally protected, whereas a mixture of speech and conduct will be shielded from interference.

Freedom of Religion

All freedoms arise from the *liberty of conscience*. In those nations that respect the *freedom to believe,* there are concomitant rights allowing expression of those beliefs (which many times entails conduct). Religion is the purest form of such beliefs. Beliefs cannot exist in a vacuum. They must be aired in the marketplace of ideas. In an early religious liberty case, *Cantwell v. Connecticut,*[2] the United States Supreme Court resolved that the protection for religion in the Constitution "embraces two concepts—freedom to believe and freedom to act. The first is absolute but in the nature of things, the second cannot be. Conduct remains subject to regulation for the protection of society."[3]

The context of this resolution arose when Jesse Cantwell, a Jehovah's Witness, was arrested for a breach of the peace on April 26, 1938. Cantwell, seeking to proselytize, approached two pedestrians on a public street and requested permission to play them a phonograph record. The record, entitled "Enemies," was a general attack upon all religious systems and was particularly caustic toward the Roman Catholic Church. The hearers were highly offended.

Despite the fact that the neighborhood where Jesse Cantwell sought to proselytize was predominantly Roman Catholic, the Supreme Court reversed his conviction. Specifically noting that Cantwell was not "noisy, truculent, overbearing or offensive," the Court stressed that "he wished only to interest [others] in his propaganda."[4] As such, in deciding this case the Supreme Court weighed two conflicting interests:

> The fundamental law declares the interest of the United States that the free exercise of religion be not prohibited and that freedom to communicate information and opinion be not abridged. The State of Connecticut has an obvious interest in the preservation and protection of peace and good order within her borders. . . . [I]n this instance . . . it has come into fatal collision with the overriding interest protected by the federal compact.[5]

In order to prohibit such activities, the Court held that a "clear and present danger to a substantial interest of the state" must be shown.[6] However, the Court cautioned that it "[i]s . . . clear that a State may by general and non-discriminatory legislation regulate the times, the places, and the manner of soliciting upon its streets, and the holding of meetings thereon."[7]

Cantwell v. Connecticut is of particular relevance for a number of reasons. First, *Cantwell* is a freedom of religion case rather than a freedom of speech case. This makes it clear that the constitutional protection of religion includes the dissemination of religious beliefs in open public forums. Second, *Cantwell* clearly asserts the "belief-action dichotomy." Belief is absolutely protected, while conduct (including religious self-expression) is granted substantial protection. Third, a state may regulate religious expression in public forums with reasonable and nondiscriminatory time, place, and manner restrictions. Fourth, the Court in *Cantwell* "borrows" the "clear and present danger" test from the speech context and applies it to religious freedom.[8]

In later cases, what is traditionally referred to as the "free exercise model" was established. The "free exercise model" makes four inquiries in any case where religious liberty is in jeopardy:

(1) Does the religious adherent have a sincere and centrally held religious belief or belief-motivated action?[9]

(2) Has the government, through some "state action," interfered with or burdened the free exercise of religion?[10]

(3) Can the state justify imposing this burden by showing a "compelling state interest" in regulating that conduct?[11]

(4) Has the state used the least restrictive means to achieve the fulfillment of that compelling state interest?[12]

Thus, in order to justify a state regulation which would interfere with the expression of religious ideas, the state must justify its actions by showing a "compelling state interest" and that the government has used the least restrictive means of protecting that government interest. This style of analysis is quite similar to modern freedom of speech analysis.

Freedom of Speech
Freedom of speech, as is the case with other First Amendment rights, is not an absolute. Few would advocate that it should be. As Justice Holmes stressed in *Schenck v. United States*[13] in 1919, "[t]he most stringent protection of free speech would not protect a man in falsely shouting fire in a theatre and causing a panic."[14] Holmes continued:

> The question in every case is whether the words used are used in such circumstances and are of such a nature as *to create a clear and present danger* that they will bring about the substantive evils that Congress has a right to prevent.[15]

Although the clear and present danger criterion is useful in cases where free speech is curtailed, modern courts more and more speak of employing a "balancing test" in such cases.[16] Simply put, "where a government restricts the speech of a private person, the state action may be sustained only if the government can show that the regulation is a precisely drawn means of serving a compelling state interest."[17] As previously noted, this is a very similar standard to that used in cases where the freedom of religion is violated.

Because of the absolute terms found in the First Amendment, certain practical problems arise. The First Amendment states in part: "Congress shall make no law . . . abridging the freedom of speech, or of the press. . . ." Certain classifications of expression are offensive to the common law and the community at large. Thus, there are narrowly limited classes of speech which may make one subject to criminal or civil sanctions. In a very real sense these categories of expression are not "speech" within the meaning of the First Amendment.[18]

The high threshold, the Supreme Court has held, necessary to enter one of these "non-speech" categories ensures that "so long as the means are peaceful, the communication need not meet standards of acceptability."[19] Those categories which the Constitution does not protect include "fighting words," obscenity, and incitement to riot or crime.

"Fighting words"—those that provoke immediate violence—are not protected by the First Amendment.[20] "Fighting words" (along with those words that create an immediate panic) are "words that may have all the effect of force."[21] This type of speech is (1) a personal insult, (2) directed at a particular group or person, (3) using "epithets likely to provoke the average person to retaliation."[22] This formula was first stated in *Chaplinsky v*

New Hampshire[23] and was later curtailed in *Terminiello v. Chicago*,[24] where the Supreme Court held:

> [A] function of free speech . . . is to invite dispute. It may indeed best serve its high purpose when it induces a condition of unrest, creates dissatisfaction with conditions as they are, or even stirs people to anger. Speech is often provocative and challenging. It may strike at prejudices and preconceptions and have profound unsettling effects as it presses for acceptance.[25]

Terminiello marked the realization that a hostile audience should not be permitted to censor an unpopular expressive activity by feigning offense at such expressions.[26]

Obscenity is not particularly relevant here. However, in passing it should be said again that speech "need not meet standards of acceptability"[27] to be protected. As such, both offensive and coercive speech are protected under the First Amendment. As the Supreme Court has recognized: "The language of the political arena, like the language in labor disputes, is often vituperative, abusive, and inexact."[28]

The last category of "non-speech" expressive activity is that of incitement to riot. Incitement does not include mere *advocacy* of the use of force or violence— *actions must be performed in the furtherance of that end.* In this respect, the Supreme Court in 1961 noted:

> [T]he mere abstract teaching . . . of the moral propriety or even moral necessity for a resort to force and violence, is not the same as preparing a group for violent action and steering it to such action.[29]

This distinction between *abstract advocacy* and "advocacy [which] is directed to inciting or producing imminent lawless action and [which] is likely to incite or produce such action"[30] permits consistency with "the profound national commitment that debate on public issues should be uninhibited, robust, and wide open."[31] Of course, as the Supreme Court has held, a "[s]tate may not unduly suppress free communication of views, religious or otherwise, under the guise of conserving desirable conditions."[32] Nor, as the Supreme Court recognized in 1951, should the objections of a hostile audience be permitted to silence a speaker:

> It is one thing to say that the police cannot be used as an instrument for the suppression of unpopular views, and another to say that, when . . . the speaker passes the bounds of argument or persuasion and undertakes incitement to riot, they are powerless to prevent a breach of the peace.[33]

The Freedom of Peaceful Assembly and to Petition for Redress of Grievances

The Supreme Court has long recognized the rights of individuals to organize in order to make their voices heard on public issues. Justice John Harlan, writing for the United States Supreme Court in *NAACP v. Alabama*,[34] commented: "Effective advocacy of both public and private points of view, particularly controversial ones, is undeniably enhanced by group association. . . . [There is a] close nexus between the freedoms of speech and assembly."[35] Moreover, as the Supreme Court had earlier established:

> [C]onsistently with the Federal Constitution, peaceable assembly for lawful discussion cannot be made a crime. The holding of meetings for peaceable political action cannot be proscribed.[36]

In fact, such activities, rather than being subversive as insinuated by some, have been a main channel for peaceful change in this country. As the Supreme Court has noted, "the practice of persons sharing common views banding together to achieve a common end is deeply embedded in the American political process."[37] For the Supreme Court, the rationale for such a "banding together" is clear:

> [B]y collective effort individuals can make their views known, when, individually, their voices would be faint or lost. The 18th Century Committees of Correspondence and the pamphleteers were early examples of this phenomena and the Federalist Papers were perhaps the most significant and lasting example.[38]

The boundaries of this freedom of association are delineated in *DeJonge v. Oregon*,[39] in which Chief Justice Charles Evan Hughes wrote:

> The question, if the rights of free speech and peaceable assembly are to be preserved, is not as to the auspices under which the meeting is held but as to its purpose; not as to the relations of the speakers, but whether their utterances transcend the bounds of the freedom of speech which the Constitution protects.[40]

This freedom of association, the Supreme Court later held, protects one from guilt by association: "The right to associate does not lose all constitutional protection merely because some members of the group may have participated in conduct or advocated doctrine that itself is not protected."[41] However, the standard for imposing liability in "association" cases is stated by the Supreme Court in *NAACP v. Claiborne Hardware*:[42]

> For liability to be imposed by reason of association alone, it is necessary to establish that the group itself possessed unlawful goals and that the individual held a specific intent to further those illegal aims.[43]

This is quite similar to the test for incitement discussed earlier.

The Right to Receive Information

In 1965 in *Lamont v. Postmaster General*[44] Justice William Brennan restated a vital need for the right to receive information:

> The dissemination of ideas would accomplish nothing if otherwise willing addressees are not free to receive and consider them. It would be a barren marketplace of ideas that had only sellers and no buyers.[45]

As one legal commentator has written: "Freedom to speak would be a hollow right if a concomitant right to hear the speech did not exist."[46]

Springing from the First Amendment right to free speech, the right to hear protects the listener. It is vital that this constitutional right be secured; otherwise a powerful government could guarantee "free speech" but restrict that speech to areas where no one could hear it. Free speech in such a setting would be a vacuous right without any meaningful validity. As a consequence, the Supreme Court has been careful to recognize in numerous cases the inherent right of individuals to receive information.[47]

Thus, the First Amendment has two basic roles. The First Amendment protects "not only . . . the role [of] . . . fostering individual self-expression but also . . . [of] . . . affording the public access to discussion, debate, and the dissemination of information and ideas."[48] This second role, protecting "the right to receive information and ideas,"[49] is equally vital to expressive freedom as the ability to speak or print, and therefore equally protected.

These principles were enunciated by the Supreme

Court in 1982 in *Board of Education, Island Trees, Etc. v. Pico,*[50] where a school board removed certain books from the school library. The Supreme Court, forbidding such censorship, resolved that the First Amendment rights of students were being violated. The Court noted that the right to receive information emanates from two sources—the sender and the recipient.[51] Regarding the sender the Court found:

> This right is an inherent corollary of the rights of free speech and press that are explicitly guaranteed in the Constitution. . . . [T]he right to receive information follows ineluctably from the *sender's* First Amendment right to send them: "The right of freedom of speech and press embraces the right to distribute literature, and necessarily protects the right to receive it."[52]

Thus the Constitution protects the right to receive information as the ineluctable corollary of the sender's right to disseminate ideas. This is the extent of a sender's protection for expression.

The second source of the right to receive information under *Board of Education, Island Trees, Etc. v. Pico* is the purported recipient. The Supreme Court found that "the right to receive ideas is a necessary predicate to the recipient's meaningful exercise of his own rights of speech, press and political freedoms."[53]

This right, the freedom of "impression," is the freedom originating *in a recipient* to receive "suitable access to *social, political, esthetic, moral and other ideas* and experiences which is crucial here. That right may not constitutionally be abridged."[54]

Conclusion

The bottom line is that expression is protected unless it crosses over into activity that traditionally has not been protected (such as the perpetration of crime). However, when expression does fall within the large area of protected activity, it is to be unfettered and free, even if society as a whole is in opposition to it. Without this guarantee free societies soon come to resemble the tyrannies the free world is presently struggling against.

Part Two

The Freedom of
Public Discourse

3

The Historical Origins of the Freedom of Expression

Freedom of speech is a *principal Pillar* in a free Government: when this support is taken away, the Constitution is dissolved, and Tyranny is erected on its ruins.

James Alexander (eighteenth-century attorney)

The liberty to speak, write, and gather together publicly has not come easy in the United States. It has been a struggle.

Freedom has been bought with the price of arrests, convictions, prison terms, and sometimes blood. It is often the dissenter (usually in the extreme minority) that forges the way for expansion of rights.

Repression can exist only in a country that has no dissent. Protection of dissent, then, becomes vital to future freedoms. Such protection has come slowly, but, then again, only because there were those who were willing to pay the price.

Fortunately, when this country had its beginnings early Americans had a basis in the fundamental laws of the old country to draw from. Thus, the British system of rights, which the colonists would later rebel against, provided a seminal charter for the later protection of the freedom of expression.

John Peter Zenger

Freedom of expression (which includes the freedoms of religion, press, and association) was not in any sense guaranteed by the English Constitution. Liberty of press, for example, was neither in the English Petition of Rights, nor in the British Bill of Rights. However, it is implied as a part of the "rights of Englishmen" which the American colonials believed were being infringed.

Censorship of printing is as old as printing itself. Indeed, one of the first decrees of the English Star Chamber held:

> Each printer must register; that no press be established outside of London save one at each great University; that the archbishop of Canterbury, the bishop of London and others were to regulate the number of presses and printers.[1]

It was against such restrictions that John Milton printed his *Areopagitica.*

Various licensing acts, libel acts, and taxes upon publication were used to limit expression of opposing viewpoints. This suppression was transplanted by colonial governors and was placed over the American colonies.[2] One such unsuccessful "tax on knowledge" was the notorious Stamp Act which our country's Founding Fathers found to be so noxious in 1766. Because of their outcry and protest, the tax was suspended.

The history of printing in Great Britain is an indispensable part of the American history of the freedom of speech. In capsulized form, Supreme Court Justice Joseph Story chronicled:

> The art of printing soon after its introduction, we are told, was looked upon, as well in England as in other countries, as merely a matter of state, and subject to the coercion of the crown. It was, therefore, regulated in

England by the king's proclamations, prohibitions, charters of privilege, and licenses, and finally by the decrees of the Court of Star-Chamber, which limited the number of printers and of presses which each should employ, and prohibited new publications, unless previously approved by proper licensers. On the demolition of this odious jurisdiction, in 1641, the Long Parliament of Charles the First, after their rupture with that prince, assumed the same powers which the Star-Chamber exercised with respect to licensing books; and during the Commonwealth (such is human frailty and the love of power even in republics!) they issued their ordinances for that purpose, founded principally upon a Star-Chamber decree in 1637. After the restoration of Charles the Second, a statute on the same subject was passed, copied, with some few alterations, from the parliamentary ordinances. The act expired in 1679, and was revived and continued for a few years after the revolution of 1688. Many attempts were made by the government to keep it in force; but it was so strongly resisted in Parliament that it expired in 1694, and has never since been revived.[3]

The law of seditious libel was, however, still viable in the colonies, and is a recurring problem throughout American constitutional history. The doctrine of seditious libel rests in the belief (under the theory of divine right of kings) that "the sovereign can do no wrong." Therefore, whenever there was "the intentional publication, without lawful excuse or justification, of written blame of any public man, or of the law, or of any institution established by law,"[4] the publisher was automatically guilty of seditious libel regardless of the truth of the publication. It was against this backdrop that the John Peter Zenger case occurred.

The trial of John Zenger in 1733 was a primary case which shaped the concept of the freedom of expression (and especially free press). Zenger, the publisher of the New York *Journal*, printed two satirical songs in derision of the governor's political party. The Council (the governor and his appointees) ordered that all copies of the *Journal* be burned. Moreover, Zenger was arrested under a warrant from the Council after the grand jury refused to indict him for libel.

Andrew Hamilton, one of the most eloquent attorneys of the colonial era, persuaded the jury at trial that it had the duty to determine the law and the facts. The jury responded with an acquittal. Previously it had been determined that a judge had sole discretion in determining whether a statement was or was not libelous. The jury could determine only the fact as to whether or not it was published.

Thus, the Zenger case established some American standards regarding libel. First, the jury determined whether a statement was libelous or not, in light of all of the surrounding circumstances. Second, the determination was made by the people, not by the "injured party" (that is, the Council). Third, truth was a defense to libel.

At any rate James Alexander, a lawyer, publisher, and supporter of Zenger, noted several years later:

> Freedom of speech is a *principal Pillar* in a free Government: when this support is taken away, the Constitution is dissolved, and Tyranny is erected on its ruins.[5]

As Professor Zechariah Chafee wrote:

> All the American cases before 1791 prove that our common law of sedition was exactly like that of England, and it would be extraordinary if the First Amendment enacted the English sedition law of that time, which was repudiated by every American and every liberal Englishman, and altered through Fox's Libel Act by Parliament itself the very next year.[6]

This gradual repudiation of the doctrine of seditious libel rested upon a new view of government. James Madison expressed it well:

> If we advert to the nature of Republican Government, we shall find that the censorial power is in the people over the Government, and not in the Government over the people.[7]

This view was earlier stated by the Continental Congress in an Address to the Inhabitants of Quebec in 1774:

> The last right we shall mention, regards the freedom of the press. The importance of this consists, besides the advancement of truth, science, morality, and arts in general, in its diffusion of liberal sentiments on the administration of Government, its ready communication of thoughts between subjects, and its consequential promotion of union among them, whereby oppressive officers are shamed or intimidated, into more honourable and just modes of conducting affairs.[8]

The Liberty Tree

A unique part of our national heritage of self-expression was the advent of the Liberty Tree, and its successor in interest, the Liberty Pole. These wooden standards were a rallying point for dissent, be it from British rule, so-called Federalist oppression, or slavery's expansionism. At various times in our nation's history, from 1652 through 1856, groups of Americans seeking to express their concerns used these devices as a symbol, a form of silent propaganda.

Arthur M. Schlesinger's *Liberty Tree: A Genealogy* is a fascinating review of over 200 years of the symbolism of Liberty Trees.[9] Schlesinger traces the term "Liberty Tree" to the original article in Boston in 1765. At the corner of Essex and Washington Streets, near the Boston Common, an elm tree became the stage for the expression of popular outrage against the Stamp Act. Upon the boughs of this original Liberty Tree Andrew Oliver, a newly commissioned stamp distributor, was hanged in effigy. Oliver later refused to take his post. Thus, within a short time this place became the rallying place for Samuel Adams and the "Sons of Liberty."

In imitation of Boston, Braintree[10] and Dedham,[11] Massachusetts, Newport, Rhode Island,[12] and Norwich, Connecticut soon established their own memorials to freedom. However, the most notable tree, besides that in Boston, was one *built* in New York on June 4, 1766.

Although christened a Liberty Tree by the colonists, New York's Liberty Tree was actually a pine mast. This mast, built to celebrate the rescinding of the Stamp Act, was deliberately placed near the British barracks on the Common.[13] On August 19 several British soldiers cut the Liberty Tree down. Shortly thereafter it became almost a contest between the British troops and the New York Sons of Liberty whether or not the pole should stand.

For example, on the night of January 26, 1770 a group of Redcoats, after having tried unsuccessfully a few evenings before, felled the Liberty Pole. The next day a mass meeting, which had originally been called to berate the Billeting Act, assembled at the scene, and 3,000 persons angrily resolved to treat any soldiers found thereafter abroad after dark "as Enemies to the Peace of this City."[14]

The following morning some regulars were discovered nailing up placards in prominent places deriding the resolutions, and this brought on a street fight in which several soldiers suffered severe wounds. Minor clashes occurred in the ensuing days. Finally British General Thomas Gage ordered his men to keep to their quarters thenceforth unless accompanied by a noncommissioned officer. This major encounter, known in history as the Battle of Golden Hill, preceded by some six weeks the Boston Massacre.[15]

Therefore, on several occasions this was a place of violence, although no deaths were reported. One New York Tory wrote that for the Americans, liberty meant little more than the "[h]appiness of Assembling in the open Air, and performing idolatrous and vociferous Acts of Worship, to a Stick of Wood, called a Liberty Pole."[16]

Indeed, the contagion of Liberty Poles spread through Shutesbury, Concord, Taunton, Middleborough, Barnstable, Granville, Vineyard Haven, Hanover, and Sandwich, Massachusetts.[17] New Hampshire shortly followed suit. The practice was later followed as far south as Savannah, Georgia, in June 1775.[18] Upon the outbreak of hostilities, the poles were quickly hewn down by the British.

So vital were these Liberty Poles as a rallying point for the colonists against British oppression that their memory lingered on from 1793 to 1796 in the form of a coin minted by the United States Government. The cent was minted bearing a Liberty Pole crowned with a liberty cap.[19]

Later, after the War for Independence, the Whiskey Rebellion and the Fries Rebellion once again caused what were now called "anarchy poles" to be raised in defiance to the federal government. Regarding the latter, Alexander Graydon noted that Liberty Poles were standing "in grand colonnade from the banks of the Delaware to those of the Susquehanna."[20] These "wooden gods of sedition," as the Federalists called them, quickly arose in opposition to the Alien and Sedition Acts in 1798. The opposition press noted that when the British authorities destroyed Liberty Poles they were tyrants, but that the Federalist authorities, though doing the same, were not tyrants because "the Sedition Law forbids our calling them so."[21]

As late as 1856 the poles were constructed by abolitionists in objection to the expansion of slavery.[22] This was the last known use to which they were put.

James Madison and Thomas Paine

Obviously the flames of freedom that burned in the colonial years were later grafted into the basic framework of American society. Eventually this early experiential struggle, as manifested in the American Revolution, culminated in the drafting of the Constitution and the Bill of Rights.

Two individuals that were affected by the historical experience in which they were living later significantly advanced the cause of free expression. These were James Madison and Thomas Paine.

Madison, often referred to as the "father" of the Constitution, was affected by an incident, while yet in his early twenties, when free expression was punished. A religious dissenter known as the Reverend Elijah Craig of the Blue Run Baptist Church was imprisoned in Culpeper County for preaching. At the trial, the state's attorney of Virginia warned the court that Baptists "were like a bed of camomile; the more they were trod, the more they would spread."[23] Craig was held in jail, but continued to preach from the window.

Later Elijah Craig repeated his preaching in Orange, Virginia, where he was again imprisoned. This time his audience included the impressionable young Mr. Madison.[24]

Because of this incident, James Madison wrote to William Bradford in 1774:

> I want again to breathe your free Air. I expect it will mend my Constitution and confirm my principles. I have indeed as good an Atmosphere at home as the Climate will allow: but have nothing to brag of as to the State and

Liberty of my Country. Poverty and Luxury prevail among all sorts: Pride, ignorance and Knavery among the Priesthood and Vice and Wickedness among the Laity. It is bad enough. But it is not the worst I have to tell you. That diabolical Hell conceived principle of persecution rages among some and to their eternal Infamy the Clergy can furnish their Quota of Imps for such business. This vexes me the most of any thing whatever. There are at this [time] in the adjacent County not less than 5 or 6 well meaning men in close Goal for publishing their religious Sentiments which in the main are very orthodox. I have neither patience to hear, talk or think of any thing relative to this matter, for I have squabbled and scolded, abused and ridiculed so long about it, to [so lit]tle purpose that I [leave you] to pity me and pray for Liberty of Conscience [to revive among us].[25]

It would be difficult to believe that this event did not greatly affect Madison's views regarding freedom of speech and religion. Less susceptible of belief would be the proposition that this experience did not affect the Bill of Rights.

In the autumn months of 1775, Thomas Paine had completed work upon *Common Sense*, the historic pamphlet which was influential on the course of the American Revolution. It is one of the great examples of free expression. The first edition, published on January 9, 1776, was, in Paine's words, "turned upon the world like an orphan to shift for itself."[26]

The second edition of *Common Sense* included an interesting article entitled an "Epistle to Quakers." The Quakers were extremely hesitant to join or in any way support the move toward independence. Paine's "Epistle to Quakers" was intended to awaken the Quaker laity from their lethargy regarding the rapidly approaching Revolution. Paine wrote:

Perhaps we feel for the ruined and insulted sufferers in all and every part of the continent, with a degree of tenderness which hath not yet made its way into some of your bosoms. But be ye sure that ye mistake not the cause and ground of your testimony. Call not coldness of the soul, religion; nor put the bigot in the place of the Christian.[27]

Although there is no way to measure the success of these arguments, if circulation means success *Common Sense* was one of the most spectacular successes upon the American continent. Because of the high cost of printing, the pamphlets were sold for the then sizable sum of two shillings. Nonetheless, within the first three months *Common Sense* sold over 120,000 copies, and eventually 500,000 copies of *Common Sense* were distributed throughout the colonies.[28]

In December of 1776 the American cause for liberty was floundering. General George Washington, the leader of the Continental Army, was beset by declining morale, depleted supplies, and a rapidly shrinking contingent of soldiers. Thomas Paine, the author of *Common Sense,* the tract which in 1775-1776 had partly spurred the colonists toward independence, then penned an article for the Pennsylvania *Journal.* The article was the first of the *Crisis Papers.* The article was so popular that within a week it was republished as a pamphlet. George Washington, after reading the article, was so deeply moved that he ordered it read to the beleaguered troops shortly before the Battle of Trenton. Its words are still relevant for today:

These are the times that try men's souls. The summer soldier and the sunshine patriot will, in this crisis, shrink from the service of his country; but he that stands it now deserves the love and thanks of man and woman. Tyranny, like hell, is not easily conquered; yet we have this consolation with us—that the harder the conflict, the more glorious the triumph. What we obtain too cheap,

we esteem too lightly: It is dearness only that gives everything its value. Heaven knows how to put a proper price
upon its goods: and it would be strange indeed if so
celestial an article as freedom should not be highly rat-
ed.[29]

Partly because of this tract, and the boost in morale
it inspired, the Americans won the victory at Trenton. A
large number of troops, whose conscription to the military had expired at the end of 1776, reenlisted on January 1, 1777, thus changing the outcome of the war.

The Alien and Sedition Acts

The Americans prevailed in the Revolution and later
chartered fundamental rights in the Constitution. However, with the presidency of John Adams, a Federalist,
came a period of American history that stifled, for a
short time, free expression. This came in the form of the
Alien and Sedition Acts, passed in 1798.[30]

Supposedly passed under the exigencies of impending war with France, these acts were never applied
against "foreign agitators," but were ready instruments
of suppression wherewith President John Adams and the
Federalists sought to eliminate political opposition. By
imprisoning opposition party leaders and writers, President Adams was nominally successful.

The Federalist leaders, shocked by the temerity of
editors who dared to criticize the national policies, at-
tributed this intolerable situation in part to the influx of
irresponsible immigrants seduced by ideas set in motion
by the French Revolution. Among these immigrants who
were suspect were such statesmen and educators as Al-
bert Gallatin, Dr. Joseph Priestley, and Thomas Cooper,
all of whose distinction in learning and public affairs did
not protect them from the scorn of the Federalists.

The Federalist remedy was devoid of subtlety. Congress enacted the Alien and Sedition Acts, which length-

ened the period of residence required for naturalization, empowered the President to deport by executive order any alien whom he regarded as dangerous, and defined as a misdemeanor any statement intended to reflect unfavorably on the President or Congress. The convictions and imprisonment of a few well-known Republican editors gave warning that the Federalist leaders intended to silence the opposition.

The harm perpetrated under the Alien and Sedition Acts lapsed with the election of Thomas Jefferson to the presidency in 1801. After Jefferson and his Democratic-Republican Party came to power, Jefferson pardoned all those convicted under these acts. He later noted in personal correspondence:

> I considered, and now consider, that law to be a nullity as absolute and palpable as if Congress had ordered us to fall down and worship a golden image. It was accordingly done in every instance, without asking what the offenders had done, or against whom they offended.[31]

The Abolitionists

The early 1800s, in particular 1833 to 1843, constituted an era of confusion for the democratic process. Historian Leon Whipple writes:

> The masses, charmed by this idea of the rule of the people, were convinced that it made small difference whether you downed the minority by ballots or by brickbats, which they understood better. This form of tyranny by majority had not been anticipated by the statesmen who expected the colder process of voting down the minority to prevail over the warmer sport of killing them.[32]

Because of the intense hatred and distrust of secret organizations during this era, anti-Catholic, anti-Masonic and anti-Mormon movements each had their turn.[33]

It was, however, the abolitionist movement which came under particular fire after 1830. During this era, every southern state except Kentucky passed laws restricting the press, speech, and discussion regarding slavery.[34]

Until approximately 1830 there was a toleration of the antislavery movements in the South. A forerunner of the American abolitionist movement, Benjamin Lundy, formed more antislavery societies in North Carolina during this early era than were established in any other state. However, this toleration would be short-lived.

Abolitionists often met with whippings, brandings, beatings, tar and featherings, and occasionally hangings merely for advocating abolitionism or for merely possessing abolitionist literature.[35] Three particular occurrences raised the national sensitivities against antislavery free speech activities and writings. The abolitionist pamphlet *Appeal to the Colored Citizens of the World* was penned by David Walker, a free black of Boston, in 1829. This and William Lloyd Garrison's newspaper, the *Liberator*, were powerful tools in the launching of the abolitionist movement.

These two publications were widely censured because of their approval of Nat Turner's slave uprising in 1831,[36] and were largely viewed as inflammatory writings intended to incite slaves to rebellion. The penalty for printing or circulating anything tending to incite slave insurrections varied from the lash to imprisonment. The death penalty was the prescribed punishment for the second or third such offense (depending upon the state). Under many such statutes mere possession of abolitionist literature, regardless of the source, was punishable by fines and imprisonment.[37] As a consequence:

By about 1828 freedom of speech against slavery was dead in the South. The lack of a law was soon remedied, and statutes appeared in almost every Southern state penalizing advocacy of abolition.[38]

Several states, not content to prohibit abolitionism in their own states, attempted to place restrictions on the North. In a much publicized incident, Governor Lumpkin of Georgia signed an act of the legislature which offered a $5,000 reward to any person who could bring publisher Lloyd Garrison to Georgia to be tried. This, in effect, was payment for the commission of the crime of kidnapping.[39]

Indeed, in his seventh annual address to Congress on December 7, 1835, President Andrew Jackson requested federal legislation to prohibit incendiary publications and to declare it "proper for Congress to take such measures as will prevent the Post-Office Department, which was designed to foster an amicable intercourse and correspondence between all members of the confederacy, from being used as an instrument of the opposite character."[40] Although much debate occurred in the House of Representatives and in the press, no federal postal censure act was ever passed.

Throughout this era the abolitionists stood firm against slavery and for the liberty to voice their opinions in speech and in the press. One such person who stood firm was Elijah Lovejoy. Lovejoy argued more for the right to oppose slavery than his actual opposition to it. Because of hostilities, Lovejoy was forced to move from his native Missouri to Alton, Illinois. As a result of the public hostility toward his writings, Lovejoy's press was destroyed on four separate occasions in Alton. Shortly before Lovejoy's death he wrote:

> I have been beset night and day at Alton. And now if I go elsewhere, violence may overtake me in my retreat, and I have no more claim to the protection of any other

community than I have upon this; and I have concluded, after consultation with my friends, and earnestly seeking the counsel of God, to remain at Alton, and here to insist on protection in the exercise of my rights. If the civil authorities refuse to protect me, I must look to God, and if I die, I have determined to make my grave in Alton.[41]

On November 6, 1837, Lovejoy was shot five times and died shortly after a mob attempting to destroy his fourth press was dispersed. Former President John Quincy Adams wrote the following day:

That an American citizen in a state whose Constitution repudiates all slavery, should die a martyr in defence of the freedom of the press, is a phenomenon in the history of this Union. Martydom was said . . . to be the only test of sincerity in religious belief. It is also the ordeal through which all great improvements in the condition of men are doomed to pass. . . . Here is the most effective portraiture of the first American martyr to the freedom of the press, and the freedom of the slave.[42]

Such antipathy toward abolitionism was not limited to the South. In Boston William Lloyd Garrison was mobbed and dragged through the streets.

Into the Twentieth Century

With the coming of the War Between the States in the 1860s, free speech in war-torn America was often suspended.[43] Chaos, of course, ruled through these years and thereafter, only to be followed by the impact of the Industrial Age in the United States. It was not until the turn of the century that free-expression challenges began reaching the forefront once again.

At the turn of the century Eugene V. Debs, a self-professed Socialist, was quite prominent in the public's eye. Debs, because of his writing and speaking skills, became the primary spokesman for socialism through labor organizations.

Beginning in 1875, Debs began his long career of unionization by reorganizing the Brotherhoods of Locomotive Firemen. After his failure to unify these groups, he moved on in 1893 to organize the American Railway Union, which participated in the Pullman strike of 1894. Ignoring a court injunction, Debs refused to order the union's striking workers to return to their posts. Debs was jailed for six months on charges of contempt of court and obstructing the mail. In and around Chicago, strikers and strike-breakers clashed, resulting in damage to railroad property. Federal troops were sent in by President Grover Cleveland to quell the violence (supposedly to insure safe passage of the mail and protect interstate commerce).

Largely because of this imprisonment, Debs gravitated toward socialism and later helped to organize the Social Democratic Party of America (1897), the Socialist Party (1901), and the Industrial Workers of the World (1905). He ran for the presidency in 1900, 1904, 1908, 1912, and 1920. In 1912 Debs polled 897,011 of the 15 million votes cast (approximately 6 percent).[44]

The last of these elections is, however, the most interesting. In 1917 Congress passed the Espionage Act,[45] and in 1918 a "sedition" amendment was added. This act, a part of the worldwide hysteria caused by the Bolshevik Revolution in Russia, prohibited any activities in opposition to the war effort in Europe (World War I).

The Espionage Act and the Sedition Act Amendment were some of the most repressive legislation ever passed by the United States government. The amendment of May 16, 1918[46] prohibited any "attempts to obstruct" the war efforts. This included "uttering, printing, writing, or publishing any disloyal, profane, scurrilous, or abusive language, or language intended to cause contempt, scorn, contumely or disrepute as regards the form of government of the United States . . . of the Constitution . . . or the flag . . . or any language intended to incite resistance to the United States or promote the cause of its enemies."[47]

In 1917 Debs wrote to Kate Richards O'Hare, who was under indictment for violating the Espionage Act: "I cannot yet believe that they will ever dare to send you to prison for exercising your constitutional rights of free speech. . . . But if they do . . . I shall feel guilty to be at large."[48]

On January 18, 1918, Debs addressed a crowd at Canton, Ohio, cataloging a list of Socialist persecutions and restating his radical views. Among his rhetoric was a charge to the audience that "you need to know that you are fit for something better than slavery and cannon fodder."[49] On June 30, 1918 he was arrested for that address. During September 1918 Debs was tried for sedition and in many instances seemed to assist the prosecution in trying to convict him. He outlined on the stand his Socialist utopia. He was, of course, convicted and was sentenced to ten years in prison.

His case went before the United States Supreme Court, and in *Debs v. United States*[50] his conviction was upheld. In response to the decision, Debs called the justices "begowned, bewhiskered, bepowdered old fossils."[51]

In 1919, during the peak of the "Palmer Raids," Debs campaigned for the office of President of the United States from his jail cell.[52] Despite the Justice Department's restriction that Debs could only send statements of 500 censored words a week, Debs received 919,000 votes.[53] In 1921 President Warren Harding pardoned Debs. Debs died in 1926.

Dissent and the Supreme Court

Debs was not alone in his violation of the Espionage Act. Arrests were numerous:

> Sections 3 and 4 resulted in a flood of prosecutions and controversy. Professor Zechariah Chafee in 1920 compiled figures which showed that at least 1,956 prosecutions involving freedom of speech had been started between June 15, 1917 and June 30, 1919, under the Espionage Act. There had been convictions in 877 cases and 285 cases were still pending in 1920. Most of these cases are unreported.[54]

Among the litigation which made its way through the federal court system, five principal cases stand out. In *Schenck v. United States*,[55] the United States Supreme Court in 1919 unanimously upheld the convictions of certain defendants who distributed circulars through the mails denouncing the draft as unconstitutional and urging the draftees to assert their rights. The "clear and present danger" test was the most notable product of Justice Oliver Wendell Holmes's decision in this case.

Abrams v. United States,[56] also a 1919 Supreme Court case, involved a group of Russian nationals who were arrested because they were pamphleteering agitation against the American deployment of troops to Vladivostok and Murmansk in Russia in 1918. (This group feared the United States would try to interfere with the Communist Revolution in Russia.) The Supreme Court upheld their convictions under the Espionage Act, finding that "the obvious effect of this appeal . . . would be to persuade persons . . . not to aid government loans and not to work in ammunition factories."[57] In the fall of 1921 these prisoners were released from prison upon the condition that they be deported to Russia.[58]

Schaefer v. United States[59] involved the convictions of

the officers of the *Philadelphia Tageblatt,* an American newspaper published in German. In this 1920 decision the Supreme Court upheld the convictions of the corporate officers responsible for the printing and publication of fifteen allegedly pro-German articles.

In *Pierce v. United States*[60] the Supreme Court, again in 1920, upheld the convictions of three Albany, New York Socialists who distributed an antiwar pamphlet entitled, "The Price We Pay," written by an Episcopal clergyman named Irwin Tucker. The offensive section stated in part:

> Our entry into [the war] was determined by the certainty that if the allies do not win, J. P. Morgan's loans to the allies will be repudiated, and those American investors who bit on his promises would be hooked.[61]

This was sufficient cause for imprisonment under the Espionage Act.

Then in 1921, in *Berger v. United States,*[62] the United States Supreme Court reversed the convictions of Irwin Tucker and Victor Berger (the editor of the *Milwaukee Leader* and a founder of the Socialist Party in the United States). Both were convicted of speaking, writing, printing, and distributing antiwar pamphlets. Trial Court Judge Landis, during the trial, made slighting remarks regarding German Americans. The convictions were set aside by the United States Supreme Court upon the basis of judicial bias. As several commentators have noted:

> Victor Berger was the first Socialist Representative elected to Congress (1911-1913). The House of Representatives twice refused to accept his credentials in 1919 and 1920, when he was returned to Congress by the voters.[63]

After the war fever of World War I ended, arrests under the Espionage Act greatly slowed only to be resurrected by the same nationalistic feelings in the wake of World War II in the form of the Smith Act. The Smith Act[64] was in essence much less restrictive than its predecessor. The Smith Act, enacted in 1940, did not forbid criticism of the United States, but did prohibit the advocacy of the use of violence and force. Although early convictions were upheld under this law, the United States Supreme Court determined that advocacy and teaching of forcible overthrow of government as an abstract principle is immune from prosecution.[65]

A Checkered History
Free expression in this country has a checkered past. As exigencies and new or different forms of dissent arose, speech, press, and other expressions were often curtailed. Many times arrests, convictions, and prison terms were the result.

It wasn't until the mid-1920s that a uniform approach was taken toward the guarantees of the First Amendment. This process, too, has a checkered past, but one that points toward greater protection for First Amendment freedoms.

4

Self-Expression in Public: The Development of a Right

> Wherever the title of streets and parks may rest, they have immemorially been held in trust for the use of the public and . . . have been used for purposes of assembly, communicating thoughts between citizens, and discussing public questions. Such use of the streets and public places has, from ancient times, been a part of the privileges, immunities, rights, and liberties of citizens. . . . [I]t must not, in the guise of regulation, be abridged or denied.
>
> *Hague v. C.I.O.*, 307 U.S. 496, 515-516 (1939)

The right of self-expression on public thoroughfares, such as public streets and parks, had a somewhat shaky beginning. However, soon after the United States Supreme Court began applying the freedoms of the Bill of Rights as restrictions on the states, the right to self-expression on public thoroughfares became entrenched as an essential liberty.

Beginnings

The vehicle for applying the First Amendment against the States through the Fourteenth Amendment was *Gitlow v. People of New York*,[1] a case decided by the United States Supreme Court in 1925. It resulted in upholding a conviction for merely printing and distributing leftist propaganda. Gitlow printed and caused to be distributed three pamphlets—"The Left Wing Manifesto," "Program of the Left Wing," and "Communist Program." In upholding the conviction the United States Supreme Court noted:

> The state cannot reasonably be required to measure the danger from every such utterance in the nice balance of a jeweler's scale. A single revolutionary spark may kindle a fire that, smouldering for a time, may burst into a sweeping and destructive conflagration.[2]

Therefore, in the first case to apply the freedom of the press against the states, the Court upheld the conviction.

However, Justices Oliver Wendell Holmes, Jr., and Louis Brandeis vigorously dissented:

> Every idea is an incitement. It offers itself for belief and if believed it is acted on unless some other belief outweights it or some failure of energy stifles the movement at its birth. The only difference between the expression of an opinion and an incitement in the narrower sense is the speaker's enthusiasm for the result. Eloquence may set fire to reason.[3]

Holmes's and Brandeis's opinion would soon carry the day.

Almost a decade later, in 1934, Dirk DeJonge was indicted for a violation of Oregon's "criminal syndicalism" statute.[4] DeJonge was sentenced to seven years imprisonment for speaking at a Communist Party rally. In his speech DeJonge protested the conditions of the city jail, commented upon the developments in a longshoreman's strike, and urged the purchase of Communist literature. While the meeting was still in progress, the hall where they were meeting was raided by the police (although the meeting was conducted in an orderly manner).

The United States Supreme Court reversed the conviction in *DeJonge v. Oregon.*[5] The Court held:

> Freedom of speech and of the press are fundamental rights which are safeguarded by the due process clause of the Fourteenth Amendment of the Federal Constitution. . . . The right of peaceable assembly is a right cognate to those of free speech and free press and is equally fundamental.[6]

Chief Justice Charles Evans Hughes, writing for the Court, explained:

> As this Court said in *United States v. Cruikshank,* 92 U.S. 542, 552: "The very idea of a government, republican in form, implies a right on the part of its citizens to meet peaceably for consultation in respect to public affairs and to petition for a redress of grievances." . . . [T]he legislative intervention can find constitutional justification only by dealing with the abuse. The rights themselves may not be curtailed. The greater the importance of safeguarding the community from incitements to the overthrow of our institutions by force and violence, the more imperative is the need to preserve inviolate the constitutional rights of free speech, free press and free assembly in order to maintain the opportunity for free political discussion, to the end that government may be responsive to the will of the people and that changes, if desired, may be obtained by peaceful means. Therein lies the security of the Republic, the very foundation of constitutional government.[7]

Thus, the holding of meetings for peaceful political actions are protected by the First Amendment and cannot be proscribed.

Jehovah's Witnesses

In *Lovell v. Griffin*[8] Alma Lovell, a Jehovah's Witness, was convicted for violating a City of Griffin, Georgia ordinance which required written permission to be obtained from the Griffin city manager prior to the distribution of literature of any kind. Lovell was arrested for distributing the publication "Golden Age" and, after defaulting payment of the $50 fine, was sentenced to fifty days in jail.

The United States Supreme Court reversed Lovell's conviction, finding the ordinance facially invalid. The Court noted:

> The struggle for the freedom of the press was primarily directed against the power of the licensor. It was against that power that John Milton directed his assault by his "Appeal for the Liberty of Unlicensed Printing." And the liberty of the press became initially a right to publish *"without* a license what formerly could be published only *with* one."[9]

The Court continued:

> The liberty of the press is not confined to newspapers and periodicals. It necessarily embraces pamphlets and leaflets. Those indeed have been historic weapons in the defense of liberty, as the pamphlets of Thomas Paine and others in our own history abundantly attest. The press in its historic connotation comprehends every sort of publication which affords a vehicle of information and opinion.[10]

The Court then found these administrative preclearances invalid.

Hague v. Committee for Industrial Organization,[11] decided in 1939, is one of the early charter cases embodying the rights of citizens in First Amendment forums.

Individual citizens, unincorporated labor organizations, and the Committee of Industrial Organizations brought a suit against the mayor of Jersey City, the Director of Public Safety, the Chief of Police, and the Board of Commissioners in federal district court, seeking an injunction. The labor union sought an injunction to restrain the Chief of Police from acting under color of law in forbidding the lease of a public hall to the union, evicting persons from the municipality because of their labor organizing activities, and through violence and force interfering with the distribution of pamphlets discussing the National Labor Relations Act. Nearly all of the contested actions occurred upon government-owned parks, streets, and sidewalks.

The United States Supreme Court upheld the granting of the injunction. Justice Owen Roberts delivered an opinion in which Justice Hugo Black concurred. In this decision, however, the basic standard for all future public park, street, and sidewalk forum cases was established. The Court held:

> Wherever the title of streets and parks may rest, they have immemorially been held in trust for the use of the public and, time out of mind, have been used for purposes of assembly, communicating thoughts between citizens, and discussing public questions. Such use of the streets and public places has, from ancient times, been a part of the privileges, immunities, rights, and liberties of citizens. The privilege of a citizen of the United States to use the streets and parks for communication of views on national questions may be regulated in the interest of all; it is not absolute but relative, and must be exercised in subordination to the general comfort and convenience, and in consonance with peace and good order; but it must not, in the guise of regulation, be abridged or denied.[12]

Justices Harlan Stone and Stanley Reed concurred in the result, while Chief Justice Hughes concurred in part. As a consequence, the injunction was upheld.

Less than one year later the United States Supreme Court again turned to administrative preclearances for the distribution of pamphlets. *Schneider v. State*[13] was a grouping of four challenged ordinances which restricted or prohibited the distribution of circulars, fliers, and pamphlets. Three of the ordinances were flat prohibitions on distribution.

In the primary case, a Jehovah's Witness distributed literature without undergoing the fingerprinting and photographing required under the licensing process. The Supreme Court overturned all four ordinances as unconstitutional:

> Municipal authorities, as trustees for the public, have the duty to keep their communities' streets open and available for movement of people and property, the primary purpose to which the streets are dedicated. So long as legislation to this end does not abridge the constitutional liberty of one rightfully upon the street to impart information through speech or the distribution of literature, it may lawfully regulate the conduct of those using the streets. For example, a person could not exercise this liberty by taking his stand in the middle of a crowded street, contrary to traffic regulations, and maintain his position to the stoppage of all traffic; a group of distributors could not insist upon a constitutional right to form a cordon across the street and to allow no pedestrian to pass who did not accept a tendered leaflet; nor does the guarantee of freedom of speech or of the press deprive a municipality of power to enact regulations against throwing literature broadcast in the streets. Prohibition of such conduct would not abridge the constitutional liberty since such activity bears no necessary relationship to the freedom to speak, write, print or distribute information or opinion. . . . This Court has characterized the freedom of speech and that of the press as fundamental personal rights and liberties. The phrase is not an empty one and was not lightly used.[14]

The Court, in answer to the state's allegation that the restrictions on pamphleteering were a reasonable regulation to control litter, found:

> We are of opinion that the purpose to keep the streets clean and of good appearance is insufficient to justify an ordinance which prohibits a person rightfully on a public street from handing literature to one willing to receive it. Any burden imposed upon the city authorities in cleaning and caring for the streets as an indirect consequence of such distribution results from the constitutional protection of the freedom of speech and press. This constitutional protection does not deprive a city of all power to prevent street littering. There are obvious methods of preventing littering. Amongst these is the punishment of those who actually throw paper on the streets.[15]

As such, all four statutes were held to be invalid.

In 1941, in *Cox v. New Hampshire*,[16] the United States Supreme Court again dealt with the right of self-expression on public thoroughfares. *Cox* concerned an appeal by five of the sixty-three Jehovah's Witnesses convicted for violating an ordinance requiring a permit before starting a parade or procession.

The Jehovah's Witnesses, numbering about eighty, lined up in a single-file procession, bearing picket signs with such inscriptions as "Religion is a snare and a racket" and "Serve God and Christ the King." The marchers interfered with the normal sidewalk travel, but no technical breach of the peace occurred.

The Court upheld the convictions, largely upon some of the rationale of *Schneider v. State*.[17] Thus, the picketers could *not* interfere with traffic. Chief Justice Charles Evans Hughes, who authored the decision, commented:

Civil liberties, as guaranteed by the Constitution, imply the existence of an organized society maintaining public order without which liberty itself would be lost in the excesses of unrestrained abuses. The authority of a municipality to impose regulations in order to assure the safety and convenience of the people in the use of public highways has never been regarded as inconsistent with civil liberties but rather as one of the means of safeguarding the good order upon which they ultimately depend.[18]

The following year, in 1942, a Jehovah's Witness brought yet another aspect of speech in a public forum to the fore. In a pique of "religious fervor" Mr. Chaplinsky became particularly vituperative. He was arrested shortly after calling a police officer a "damned racketeer" and a "damned fascist." Chaplinsky was convicted under a statute forbidding "fighting words."

In upholding the conviction, the United States Supreme Court, in *Chaplinsky v. New Hampshire*,[19] noted:

It has been well observed that such utterances are no essential part of any exposition of ideas, and are of such slight social value as a step to truth that any benefit that may be derived from them is clearly outweighed by the social interest in order and morality. Resort to epithets or personal abuse is not in any proper sense communication of information or opinion safeguarded by the Constitution, and its punishment as a criminal act would raise no question under that instrument.[20]

The Court in stressing the reason the conviction must be upheld wrote: "[D]amned racketeer and damned fascist are epithets likely to provoke the average person to retaliation, and thereby cause a breach of the peace."[21] Thus, Chaplinsky's conviction stood.

In 1942 and 1943 the Supreme Court first faced the issue of commercial handbilling and pamphleteering. In *Valentine v. Chrestensen,*[22] the Court determined that purely commercial advertising through handbills was *not* protected in the thoroughfares.

Later, in 1943 in *Jamison v. Texas,*[23] a Jehovah's Witness was arrested for violating a Dallas, Texas, ordinance proscribing the distribution of handbills in conjunction with solicitation. Jamison was tried for distributing "Peace, Can It Last," a Watchtower publication, and for seeking donations to pay for the cost of the pamphlet. The Supreme Court held:

> The [state] may not prohibit the distribution of handbills in the pursuit of a clearly religious activity merely because the handbills invite the purchase of books for the improved understanding of the religion to promote the raising of funds for religious purposes.[24]

In a parallel case, *Largent v. Texas,*[25] also decided in 1943, a Paris, Texas ordinance forbidding the selling or soliciting of orders for books, wares, or merchandise without a permit was determined to be "administrative censorship in an extreme form."[26]

Murdock v. Pennsylvania

Murdock v. Pennsylvania,[27] a landmark 1943 case, applied similar considerations to a flat-rate license tax on the distribution of literature. Mr. Murdock and several other Jehovah's Witnesses challenged the tax as a violation of freedom of religion, speech, and press. The Court focused on the activity of distributing literature for cost:

> It is more than preaching; it is more than distribution of religious literature. It is a combination of both. Its purpose is as evangelical as the revival meeting. This form of religious activity occupies the same high estate under the First Amendment as do worship in the churches and preaching from the pulpits. It has the same claim to

protection as the more orthodox and conventional exercises of religion. It also has the same claim as the others to the guarantees of freedom of speech and freedom of the press.[28]

The Court, drawing upon the precedents established in *Jamison* and *Valentine,* resolved:

[T]he mere fact that the religious literature is "sold" by itinerant preachers rather than "donated" does not transform evangelism into a commercial enterprise. . . . It should be remembered that the pamphlets of Thomas Paine were not distributed free of charge.[29]

Justice William O. Douglas, writing for the Court, held that the flat-rate tax was unconstitutional:

A license tax certainly does not acquire constitutional validity because it classifies the privileges protected by the First Amendment along with the wares and merchandise of hucksters and peddlers and treats them all alike. Such equality in treatment does not save the ordinance. Freedom of press, freedom of speech, freedom of religion are in a preferred position.[30]

Also decided in 1943 was the case of *Martin v. Struthers.*[31] The case originated from a challenge to an ordinance forbidding any person to knock on doors, ring doorbells, or otherwise summon to the door the occupants of any residence for the purpose of distributing to them handbills or circulars. Martin, a Jehovah's Witness, was convicted and fined ten dollars for a violation of the ordinance. Justice Hugo Black, the author of the opinion, wrote:

The ordinance does not control anything but the distribution of literature, and in that respect it substitutes the judgment of the community for the judgment of the individual householder. It submits the distributer to criminal punishment for annoying the person on whom he calls, even though the recipient of the literature distributed is in fact glad to receive it.[32]

Black continued:

Freedom to distribute information to every citizen wherever he desire to receive it is so clearly vital to the preservation of a free society that, putting aside reasonable police and health regulations of time and manner of distribution, it must be fully preserved. The dangers of distribution can be so easily controlled by traditional legal methods, leaving to each householder the full right to decide whether he will receive strangers as visitors, that stringent prohibition can serve no purpose but that forbidden by the Constitution, the naked restriction of the dissemination of ideas.[33]

Accordingly, the ordinance was invalidated as being unconstitutional.

In 1944, *Prince v. Massachusetts*[34] involved Sarah Prince's appeals of convictions for violation of Massachusetts child labor laws. Prince, a Jehovah's Witness, was the aunt and custodian of Betty M. Simmons, a nine-year-old girl. Prince was charged for a violation of the law after the child was seen selling issues of *Watchtower* magazine and for "consolation" on a public thoroughfare (while with Prince). After studying the issues involved, the Supreme Court held:

It is true children have rights, in common with older people, in the primary use of highways. But even in such use streets afford dangers for them not affecting adults. And in other uses, whether in work or in other things, this difference may be magnified. This is so not only when children are unaccompanied but certainly to some extent when they are with their parents. . . . We think that with reference to the public proclaiming of religion, upon the streets and in other similar public places, the power of the state to control the conduct of children reaches beyond the scope of its authority over adults, as is true in the case of other freedoms, and the rightful boundary of its power has not been crossed in this case.[35]

Prince's free exercise and free speech challenges were insufficient to overcome the validity of the statute.

A tax similar to that in *Murdock* was challenged in *Follett v. Town of McCormick*.[36] Follett, also a Jehovah's Witness, challenged the provisions of the McCormick ordinance which levied a flat-rate license tax upon all businesses, occupations, and professions including agents selling books. Follett refused to obtain the license. The sales of Watchtower Bible and Tract Society publications was Follett's sole source of income and support. As the Supreme Court held:

> Freedom of religion is not merely reserved for those with a long purse. Preachers of the more orthodox faiths are not engaged in commercial undertakings because they are dependent on their calling for a living. . . . The exaction of a tax as a condition to the exercise of the great liberties guaranteed by the First Amendment is as obnoxious . . . as the imposition of a censorship or a previous restraint. . . . For, to repeat, "the power to tax the exercise of a privilege is the power to control or suppress its enjoyment."[37]

An important case was *Thomas v. Collins*.[38] In *Thomas* a Texas statute required labor organizers to register with and to acquire an organizer's card from a state official before soliciting union membership. Thomas, the president of U.A.W. and vice-president of C.I.O., was to be a keynote speaker at a mass meeting on September 23, 1943, at which the Oil Workers Industrial

Union (a C.I.O. affiliate), sought to organize the employees of a Humble Oil and Refining Company plant near Houston, Texas. Six hours before Thomas was scheduled to speak, he was served with a court order restraining him.

Thomas, however, spoke and openly solicited the audience for membership in the union. He was later charged with contempt of court. Justice Wiley Rutledge wrote:

> Choice on that border, now as always delicate, is perhaps more so where the usual presumption supporting legislation is balanced by the preferred place given in our scheme to the great, the indispensable democratic freedoms secured by the First Amendment. . . . That priority gives those liberties a sanctity and a sanction not permitting dubious intrusions. And *it is the character of the right, not of the limitation, which determines what standard governs the choice.*
>
> For these reasons any attempt to restrict those liberties must be justified by clear public interest, threatened not doubtfully or remotely, but by clear and present danger. . . . Only the gravest abuses, endangering paramount interests, give occasion for permissible limitation. It is therefore in our tradition to allow the widest room for discussion, the narrowest range for its restriction, particularly when the right is exercised in conjunction with peaceable assembly. It was not by accident or coincidence that the rights to freedom in speech and press were coupled in a single guaranty with the rights of the people peaceably to assemble and to petition for redress of grievances. All these, though not identical, are inseparable. They are cognate rights . . . and therefore are united in the First Article's [sic] assurance.[39]

Even though the activities of soliciting union membership was clearly prohibited by the restraining order, the contempt charge could not be upheld.

Public Parks

Niemotko v. Maryland,[40] in 1951, involved two members of the Jehovah's Witnesses who were arrested for disorderly conduct because they held public meetings in the city park of Havre de Grace, Maryland. Although no ordinance existed regarding use of the park, it was the custom of groups seeking to use the park to obtain permits from the Park Commissioner. The Jehovah's Witnesses attempted to obtain a permit but were refused. The United States Supreme Court noted:

> The only question asked of the Witnesses at the hearing pertained to their alleged refusal to salute the flag, their views on the Bible, and other issues irrelevant to unencumbered use of the public parks. The conclusion is inescapable that the use of the park was denied because of the City Council's dislike for or disagreement with the Witnesses or their views.[41]

The Court concluded:

> It thus becomes apparent that the lack of standards in the license-issuing "practice" renders that practice a prior restraint in contravention of the Fourteenth Amendment, and that the completely arbitrary and discriminatory refusal to grant the permits was a denial of equal protection.[42]

Kunz v. New York[43] was one of the few religious speech cases *not* involving the Jehovah's Witnesses. Carl Jacob Kunz was an ordained Baptist minister and director of Outdoor Gospel Work. He had been preaching about six years under the conviction that he should "go out on the highways and byways and preach the word of God."[44]

In 1946 Kunz applied for and received a permit under a New York City ordinance which made it unlawful to hold public worship meetings without first obtaining a permit from the city police commissioner. In November of 1946 his permit was revoked because he had ridiculed and denounced other religious beliefs.[45]

The United States Supreme Court, relying upon *Hague v. C.I.O.,*[46] invalidated the entire scheme of restriction:

> It is sufficient to say that New York cannot vest restraining control over the right to speak on religious subjects in an administrative official where there are no appropriate standards to guide his action.[47]

Speech Restrictive Regulations

The question of commercial speech through pamphleteering was again addressed in 1951 when a manager of a magazine subscription canvassing campaign challenged an Alexandria, Louisiana "Green River ordinance"[48] which prohibited canvassing to solicit sales. In *Breard v. Alexandria*[49] the Supreme Court upheld the validity of such an ordinance:

> It would be, it seems to us, a misuse of the great guarantees of free speech and free press to use those guarantees to force a community to admit the solicitors of publications to the home premises of its residents.[50]

Thus, the *commercial / non-commercial* categorization was recognized as a valid distinction.

Fowler v. Rhode Island,[51] decided by the United States Supreme Court in 1953, again involved a Jehovah's Witness challenge to speech restrictive regulations. In *Fowler,* a Pawtucket ordinance permitted assembly by religious bodies in public parks, but prohibited any form of public address. Fowler was arrested for violating this ordinance while giving an address entitled "The Pathway to Peace." The address was given over two loudspeakers. The Supreme Court found one particular concession by the State of Rhode Island determinative:

Catholics could hold mass in Slater Park and Protestants could conduct their church services there without violating the ordinance. Church services normally entail not only singing, prayer, and other devotionals, but preaching as well. Even so, those services would not be barred by the ordinance. That broad concession, made in oral argument, is fatal to Rhode Island's case. For it plainly shows that a religious service of Jehovah's Witnesses is treated differently than a religious service of other sects. That amounts to the state preferring some religious groups over this one.[52]

The convictions, therefore, were overturned as violative of the First and Fourteenth Amendments.

In the same year, 1953, the Supreme Court in *Poulos v. New Hampshire*[53] faced similar regulations on public parks. In *Poulos,* however, the Supreme Court, in a rather confusing decision, found the regulations to be valid.

Jehovah's Witnesses sought to conduct religious services in a public park in Portsmouth, New Hampshire. They offered to pay all proper fees and charges and complied with all procedural requirements necessary. Although the license was refused, Poulos held services until his arrest. The ordinance left to the licensing officials no discretion, no power to discriminate, and no control over speech. In light of these facts the Court concluded:

Our Constitution does not require that we approve the violation of a reasonable requirement for a license to speak in public parks because an official error occurred in refusing a proper application.[54]

As a result the Court found the regulation valid and the infringment remediable by the judicial processes of appeal through the state courts.

Village of Schaumberg

Two recent cases involving door-to-door canvassing are *Hynes v. Mayor of Oradell*[55] and *Schaumberg v. Citizens for a Better Environment.*[56] These cases further extend the freedom of self-expression on public thoroughfares.

In the first of these, *Hynes v. Mayor of Oradell,*[57] an ordinance prohibited solicitation and door-to-door canvassing without a permit. Exceptions were made for a recognized charitable cause, or any person desiring to canvass, solicit, or call from house to house for a federal, state, county, or municipal political campaign or cause. Those who fit these categories were required to notify the police in writing rather than to get a permit. Because the statute did not define the terms "recognized charitable cause" or federal, state, county, or municipal "cause," the statute was unconstitutionally vague. "[M]en of common intelligence," the Supreme Court held, "must necessarily guess at its meaning."[58]

In the latter case, *Schaumberg v. Citizens for a Better Environment,*[59] the village of Schaumberg passed an ordinance prohibiting on-the-street and door-to-door solicitation by any charitable organization which did not use 75 percent of its receipts for charitable purposes. CBE (a nonprofit environmentalist group) challenged the constitutionality of the ordinance. The Court found:

> The issue before us, then, is not whether charitable solicitations in residential neighborhoods are within the protections of the First Amendment. It is clear they are.[60]

The village of Schaumberg proffered several justifications for the prohibition. The first of these was to prevent fraud. The Supreme Court, however, responded:

The Village's legitimate interest in preventing fraud can be better served by measures less intrusive than a direct prohibition on solicitation. Fraudulent misrepresentations can be prohibited and the penal laws used to punish such conduct directly.[61]

Regarding the householder's right to privacy the Court noted:

The ordinance is not directed to the unique privacy interests of persons residing in their homes because it applies not only to door-to-door solicitation, but also to solicitation on "public streets and public ways."[62]

Conclusion

The United States Supreme Court has made it abundantly clear that the freedom of expression on public thoroughfares can be restricted only where there has occurred the "gravest abuses." Thus, the free flow of information to other members of society must be uninhibited.

Very few would quarrel with the fact that such should be true in the cases and factual situations discussed in this chapter. However, there are those who believe free expression should be curtailed where it is highy controversial or distasteful. But, as we shall see, even the outer limits of free expression are protected under our constitutional scheme.

5

The Outer Limits of Expression

Shall we give a hearing to those who hate and despise
freedom, to those who, if they had the power would
destroy our institution? Certainly, yes! Our action must
be guided, not by their principles, but by ours.[1]

Alexander Meiklejohn

Freedom of speech, as we have seen, is often afforded to those groups which, if they were in power,
would not be quite so generous with others. However,
this can never be the standard. Free expression would
cease if speech and speech-related activities were condi-
tioned on its acceptance by others (even the majority).

Speech, to be free, must be unfettered even though
it is unpopular or distasteful. The people cannot, without limits, give over to government the power to pick
and choose what it believes to be appropriate "free"
speech. If this were the case, all speech, as history teach-
es, would be subject to state-imposed silence.

Therefore, free societies permit extremes and
fringe speech. This is speech which touches the outer
limits of the First Amendment.

Some "Extremes"

Street v. New York,[2] decided by the United States Supreme
Court in 1969, involved the burning of an American

flag in response to the slaying of a black civil rights leader. While Mr. Street burned his own flag, a crowd looked on. Police arrived and heard Street say, "We don't need no damn flag."[3] Street's actions were in violation of a New York law which forbade one to publicly "mutilate, deface, defile or defy, trample upon, or cast contempt upon, either by words or act,"[4] the flag.

The Supreme Court, in deciding the case, held the statute invalid because expression extends to "the right to differ as to things that touch the heart of the existing order."[5] This right to differ, then, includes the right to make publicly contemptuous statements about the American flag.

The Court specifically held that the New York law was overbroad in that it included both "words" and "acts" within its prohibitions. Since the police arrived only in time to hear Street shout, "we don't need no damn flag," his speech was the basis of the conviction. (They had not seen him "torch" the flag.) Hence, the statute and his conviction were invalid.

Brandenburg v. Ohio,[6] also decided by the Supreme Court in 1969, is a similar case. In *Brandenburg* the State of Ohio was attempting to convict a leader of the Invisible Empire of the Ku Klux Klan, under the Ohio Syndicalism Statute. Brandenburg, dressed in full Klan regalia, was filmed stating:

> We're not a revengent [sic] organization, but if our President, our Congress, our Supreme Court, continues to suppress the white, Caucasian race, it's possible that there might have to be some revengence [sic] taken.[7]

Besides other derogatory epithets, that was the sum of the evidence.

Citing *Dennis v. United States*[8] and *Noto v. United States,*[9] the Supreme Court invalidated the Ohio statute.

The Court noted that advocacy could not be proscribed unless "such advocacy is directed to inciting or producing imminent lawless action and is likely to incite or produce such action."[10] Because of this, the abstract teaching of a resort to force could not be prohibited.[11]

The 1974 Supreme Court decision in *Smith v. Goguen*[12] involved a Massachusetts law which penalized anyone who "publicly treats [an American flag] contemptuously."[13] In this case the defendant sewed a small cloth flag to the seat of his pants. The Supreme Court reversed his conviction and invalidated the Massachusetts state law as being void because of vagueness. Justice Lewis Powell found that the statute failed to give fair notice as to what activities were prohibited.

Spence v. Washington,[14] another 1974 Supreme Court decision, was a somewhat analogous case involving a Kent State University student who on May 10, 1970 hung an American flag upside down with a peace symbol of black tape temporarily affixed to it. The defendant did this to protest the invasion of Cambodia. The court struck down the "contemptuous use" statute because the defendant was engaged in constitutionally protected First Amendment activities. The Court noted several factors in its decision: (1) the flag was not permanently disfigured; (2) the flag was privately owned; (3) the flag was on private property; and (4) there was no risk of breach of the peace.

Village of Skokie

That free speech and expressive conduct are afforded protection even for those ideas that are hateful to us is nowhere more clearly illustrated than in the case of *Village of Skokie v. National Socialist Party of America.*[15]

Skokie, a Chicago suburb, has a population of approximately 70,000 people, 40,500 of which are Jewish. Of the Jewish population, an estimated 5,000 to 7,000 are survivors of German concentration camps. It was in this sensitive environment that Frank Collin and his group of Nazi followers insisted upon marching in 1977, in full military regalia, bearing picket signs and placards.[16] Collin's intent was to march with thirty to fifty of his followers in single file, back and forth in front of the Skokie village hall, at the heart of Skokie.

As a consequence of this, a counterdemonstration of approximately 12,000 to 15,000 persons was scheduled by the Jewish community for the same day (March 20, 1977). Moreover, the mayor of Skokie invoked three ordinances which: (1) required any demonstrators to obtain $50,000 in property damage insurance and $300,000 in liability insurance, against any possible violence that might occur;[17] (2) prohibited the display of any symbol which would intentionally foster hatred on the basis of race, religion, or national origin;[18] and, (3) permitted the village council to prohibit any demonstrations performed wearing military-style uniforms.[19] These ordinances were later ruled unconstitutional in a federal court.[20]

The village of Skokie, after a hearing of the council, sought and obtained an injunction against Collin and his group, forbidding the demonstration upon the basis that the residents would become violent. In his defense Collin argued free speech and prior restraint doctrines, to no avail. After attempting an appeal to the Illinois Appellate Court, the case was to receive a hearing, but the appellate court denied Collin's petition for a stay pending the appeal. An emergency appeal was asked and granted by the United States Supreme Court.[21] The United States Supreme Court decided that "[i]f a State seeks to impose a restraint of this kind, it must provide strict procedural safeguards . . . including immediate appellate review. . . . Absent such review, the State must instead allow a stay."[22]

A short time thereafter, the Illinois Court of Appeals reversed the injunction in part, but upheld that portion which prohibited the display of the swastika,[23] upon the basis of the "fighting words" doctrine.

On January 27, 1978 the Illinois Supreme Court held that the ban upon wearing and displaying swastikas was unconstitutional:[24]

> The display of the swastika, as offensive to the principles of a free nation as the memories it recalls may be, is symbolic political speech intended to convey to the public the beliefs of those who display it. It does not, in our opinion, fall within the definition of "fighting words."[25]

The Illinois Supreme Court resolved:

> We accordingly, albeit reluctantly, conclude that the display of the swastika cannot be enjoined under the fighting-words exception to free speech, nor can anticipation of a hostile audience justify the prior restraint. Furthermore, [previous cases] direct the citizens of Skokie that it is their burden to avoid the offensive symbol if they can do so without unreasonable inconvenience.[26]

As an epilogue it should be noted that the Nazis did not march in Skokie. The Nazis shifted their march to Chicago and demonstrated on June 24 and July 9, 1978, without serious incident.[27]

Jean Caffey Lyles concluded the matter quite cogently:

> We need to be remined how deeply and indelibly the horrors of Nazi Germany are burned into the consciousness and memories of Jewish people, how vulnerable they feel to the possibility of "another Holocaust." Skokie has done that. We need also to be reminded how fragile and tenuous our commitment is to the First Amendment guarantees of free speech and assembly,

and we are dealing not with bloodless abstractions but with the flesh-and-blood case of an obnoxious individual's or group's right to express ideals totally offensive to all the decent folk in our communities. Skokie is a disturbing symbol to remind us that the shallowness of our commitment to those principles could ultimately jeopardize the rights of all of us.[28]

Part Three

The Right to Picket

Public issue picketing, "an exercise of . . . basic constitutional rights in their most pristine and classic form" . . . has always rested on the highest rung of the hierarchy of First Amendment values.

Carey v. Brown,
447 U.S. 455, 466-467 (1980)

6

Picketing: The Historical Perspective

Picketing . . . embraces nearly every practicable, effective means whereby those interested . . . may enlighten the public. . . . [T]he safeguarding of these means is essential to the securing of an informed and educated public opinion with respect to a matter which is of public concern.

Thornhill v. Alabama,
310 U.S. 88, 104 (1940)

The right to picket, now recognized as a part of constitutional law, historically arose out of hostile origins. Indeed, further removed from "pure speech," the conduct-related activity of picketing was not only unprotected from governmental intrusion but, until 1842, was illegal per se.

The word "picketing" derives its name from military terminology. Historically a "picket" is a soldier or a group of soldiers on a line forward of the position of the main contingency of soldiers to warn against an enemy advance. Because of this, until relatively recent times negative connotations permeated court decisions concerning picketing. For example, in one case, the mere use of the word "picket" was held sufficient justification for granting an injunction against that activity.[1]

As a consequence of these negative overtones, picketers, boycotters, union organizers, and strikers were

subject to criminal indictments for alleged unlawful con-
spiracies. As late as 1905 a federal court found "there is
and can be no such thing as peaceful picketing, any
more than there can be chaste vulgarity, or peaceful
mobbing, or lawful lynching."[2] Fortunately, such an unconstitutional view of picketing was later refuted.

Picketing as Legitimate Activity

In the transformation toward legitimacy, *Commonwealth
u. Hunt*[3] was a threshold case. For the first time the
stigma of illegal conspiracy was lifted. As this Massachusetts court held:

> We think, therefore, that *associations may be entered into,
> the object of which is to adopt measures that may have a
> tendency to impoverish another, that is, to diminish his gains
> and profits,* and yet so far from being criminal or unlaw-
> ful, *the object may be highly meritorious and public spirited.*[4]

Although *Commonwealth u. Hunt* did not expressly
deal with picketing, the reasoning used there was later
extended to "persuasion" by the United States Supreme
Court in 1921 in *American Steel Foundries u. Tri-City
Council.*[5] In this case the Supreme Court seemingly
chided a lower court for recognizing "that which bears
the sinister name of picketing" as legal.[6] "The name
'picket,' " the Supreme Court concluded, "indicated a
militant purpose, inconsistent with peaceable persuasion."[7] The Court then hesitantly distinguished between
picketing as "peaceful persuasion" and picketing cam-
paigns "of . . . intimidating character."[8] Thus, with re-
luctance the Supreme Court, following the lead of the
state courts, permitted small-scale peaceful picketing.

This shift from unlawful to lawful picketing was
largely due to the influence of Justice Oliver Wendell
Holmes, Jr. In 1894 Holmes conducted the first real

analysis of picketing in his paper *Privilege, Malice, and Intent.*[9] This analysis was followed by Justice Holmes's (while sitting on the Massachusetts Supreme Court) dissenting opinions in *Vegelahn v. Gunter* (1896)[10] and *Plant v. Woods* (1900),[11] which for decades provided the judiciary with a theoretical basis for picketing cases. Early jurists referred to these writings as the "fountainhead" of modern theory.[12]

In these early cases Holmes argued that picketing was legal and in fact beneficial. He presented an analogy between the right to picket and free competition in business. Holmes stated that early decisions deciding picketing cases "turn in part on the assumption that the patrol necessarily carries with it a threat of bodily harm. That assumption I think is unwarranted."[13]

The acceptability of picketing was slowly growing. Indeed, by 1937 the United States Supreme Court held labor picketing legal, even in an instance where local sympathy was with the owner of a one-man family store.[14] At any rate, by 1938 picketing was viewed as primarily an appeal to consumers and as advertising rather than as an invitation to violence.[15]

It is interesting to note that the earliest reported case directly addressing picketing, *Gilbert v. Mickle,*[16] did not arise in the labor context. In this New York case a mayor, seeking to enforce a municipal ordinance, used picketing as the medium to warn potential customers of "mock auctions" allegedly carried on at a local auction parlor. *Gilbert v. Mickle,* reported in 1846, preceded the earliest labor picketing case by forty-two years.

Justice Louis Brandeis, in one of his seminal dissenting opinions,[17] cited *Sherry v. Perkins*[18] (1888) as the earliest labor picketing case. Thus the roots of public-issue picketing run deeper into our nation's history than does private-issue (labor) picketing. This distinction is relevant, as we shall see later.

Thornhill v. Alabama

In this early era a shift is evident. Beginning with state court decisions and gradually permeating the federal court cases, the law hesitantly changed from viewing picketing as illegal per se toward allowing small-scale peaceful picketing.

The breakthrough, in terms of widespread protection of picketing, came in 1940 in *Thornhill u Alabama*.[19] In this case the United States Supreme Court, by way of the Fourteenth Amendment, expanded federal constitutional protection to labor picketing activities.

The Supreme Court in *Thornhill* held unconstitutional an Alabama statute which prohibited the picketing of "the works or place of business" of others. The Court emphasized the free-speech nature of picketing in stating:

> Picketing or loitering or otherwise embraces nearly every practicable, effective means whereby those interested . . . may enlighten the public. . . . The safeguarding of these means is essential to the securing of an informed and educated public opinion with respect to a matter which is of public concern.[20]

The "right to receive inormation" was a central tenet of *Thornhill*. Because of this, First Amendment activities (which would include picketing) can be restricted only under exceptional circumstances. The Supreme Court held:

> Abridgement of the liberty of such discussion can be justified only where the clear danger of substantive evils arises under circumstances affording no opportunity to test the merits of ideas by competition for acceptance in the market of public opinion.[21]

The Court then carefully distinguished the situation in *Thornhill* from that in *American Foundries v. Tri-*

City Council.[22] The Court noted: "We are not now concerned with picketing *en masse,*"[23] as was the case in *American Foundries.*

Thus, by 1940 picketing had passed through several stages of development. The earliest era found courts hostile toward picketing. It was regarded illegal per se and as a criminal conspiracy. During the next stage picketing was permitted, but the courts were hesitant to extend any protection to this activity. The current stage, ushered in by *Thornhill v Alabama,* protects picketing as a form of speech-related conduct.

Therefore, between 1921 *(American Steel Foundries v Tri-City Council)* and 1940 *(Thornhill v Alabama)* a remarkable shift had occurred. Picketing, rather than being barely permitted, had been elevated to the status of a protected freedom. The question, however, is whether picketing fits within that special constitutional category known as "preferred freedoms."

A preferred freedom is one that carries a special status of protection.[24] For example, in 1943 in *Murdock v Pennsylvania,*[25] the Supreme Court made it clear that certain rights are preferred: "Freedom of press, freedom of speech, freedom of religion are in a preferred position"[26] in the scheme of constitutional protections.

Picketing, however, does not rise to this special status of constitutional protection. Because conduct is intertwined with speech elements, it is not "pure speech." The conduct is subject to greater regulation than that to which "pure speech" is subject. In certain instances picketing has been viewed by the United States Supreme Court as "an exercise of . . . basic constitutional rights in their most pristine and classical form,"[27] while in similar circumstances it is slighted as "conduct of a totally different character."[28] The precise level of protection which picketing is afforded is determined by a spectrum of variables not appropriate for discussion here.

Conclusion

Between the years 1921 and 1963 a gradual historical shift occurred. A progression of acceptability occurred which may be divided into separate stages.

First, from the early 1900s until 1921 the shift advanced picketing from being a prohibited activity to a permitted one. From 1921 until 1940 the shift continued unabated, raising the status of this activity from a permitted conduct to a protected form of self-expression. Between 1940 and the present, picketing has gained judicial and public acceptance. Thus, although it has not reached the stature of a "preferred freedom," picketing is nonetheless protected by the Constitution.

7

Picketing as Free Expression: The Modern Development

> Every expression of opinion on matters that are important has the potentiality of inducing action in the interests of one rather than another group in society. But the group in power at any moment may not impose penal sanctions on peaceful and truthful discussion on matters of public interest merely on a showing that others may thereby be persuaded to take action inconsistent with its interest.
>
> *Thornhill v. Alabama,*
> 310 U.S. 88, 104 (1940)

Picketing is, in a real sense, a conglomeration of all of the rights contained in the First Amendment. Picketing involves freedom of religion, freedom of speech and the press, freedom of assembly and association, and of course the freedom to petition the government for the redress of grievances.

Picketing, however, is a *combination* of speech and conduct and thus, as previously discussed, is not "pure speech." As such, it does not rise to the same level of protection as does "pure speech." Moreover, the level of protection will depend upon the circumstances surrounding the activity. Because picketing is a mixture of speech and nonspeech elements, it has been termed "speech-*plus*." The *"plus"* is conduct which the pickets may trigger independent of the message on the placards or whatever oral activity may accompany the picketing.

"Speech-plus"

In *Cox v. Lousiana*[1] the Supreme Court emphatically rejected the proposition that the United States Constitution granted "the same kind of freedom to those who would communicate ideas by conduct such as patrolling, marching and picketing on streets and highways, as [the First and Fourteenth] amendments afford to those who communicate ideas by pure speech."[2] Simply put, conduct is subject to regulation, whereas speech is not.

This concept may have originated with Justice William O. Douglas's 1942 concurring opinion in *Baker Driver's Local v. Wohl*.[3] There Douglas wrote:

> Picketing by an organized group is more than free speech, since it involves patrol of a particular locality and since the very presence of a picket line may induce action of one kind or another, quite irrespective of the nature of the idea being disseminated. Hence those aspects of picketing make it the subject of restrictive regulation.[4]

Although the speech elements of picketing are protected, certain other aspects of it may be subject to greater regulation.

The test which the United States Supreme Court has devised to determine whether the speech elements or the conduct elements are predominant was stated in *United States v. O'Brien*.[5] O'Brien, a war protester, was arrested for burning his draft card in a demonstration. O'Brien claimed that his conduct was a form of "symbolic speech" and therefore protected under the First Amendment. In *O'Brien* the Supreme Court held:

> We cannot accept the view that an apparently limitless variety of conduct can be labeled "speech" whenever the person engaging in the conduct intends thereby to express an idea. . . . [W]hen "speech" and "non-speech"

elements are combined in the same course of conduct, a sufficiently important governmental interest in regulating the non-speech element can justify incidental limitations on First Amendment freedoms.[6]

Finding a substantial government interest in the integrity of the draft registration system, the Court upheld O'Brien's conviction. In terms of picketing cases, this means that the objectives and intent of the picketers may determine whether the conduct elements outweigh the speech elements.

"Unlawful Immediate Objective"

Thornhill v. Alabama[7] arose when Byron Thornhill, a striking union member, told a fellow employee that the union was "on strike and did not want anybody to go up there to work."[8] Because of this, and since he was a member of a peaceful picket line, Thornhill was convicted under an Alabama statute which forbade all communications by anyone attempting to interfere with a lawful business near the business's location.

In a near-unanimous 1940 decision the United States Supreme Court in *Thornhill* overturned Thornhill's conviction and held the Alabama statute invalid. Justice Murphy, writing for the Court, held:

> Every expression of opinion on matters that are important has the potentiality of inducing action in the interests of one rather than another group in society. But the group in power at any moment may not impose penal sanctions on peaceful and truthful discussion on matters of public interest merely on a showing that others may thereby be persuaded to take action inconsistent with its interest.[9]

The Court, applying the "clear and present danger" test, failed to find any interest which could justify "affording no opportunity to test the merits of ideas by

competition for acceptance in the market of public opinion."[10]

The expansive protections granted picketing were,
however, short-lived. In the next two decades the Court
handed down eleven decisions attempting to curtail the
broad pronouncements in *Thornhill.*[11]

The first of these decisions, *Giboney v. Empire Storage
& Ice Co.,*[12] arose when a union sought to pressure the
Empire Storage & Ice Company into an exclusive dealing agreement with its members. The ice and coal drivers' union was charged with creating an illegal restraint
of trade under a Missouri statute. The picketing in that
case was unanimously found by the Supreme Court in
1949 to "[e]ffectuate the purposes of an unlawful combination, and their sole, *unlawful immediate objective* was to
induce Empire to violate the Missouri law by acquiescing
in unlawful demands to agree not to sell ice to nonunion
peddlers."[13]

The Supreme Court, applying the "unlawful immediate objective" test, emphasized the nature of the Missouri statute. This statute, unlike the law involved in
Thornhill, was not designed to restrict expression, but
rather to prevent restraint of trade. The statute in *Empire Storage* curtailed freedom of expression in picketing
only as an incidence of the legislation. Therefore, it was
not the picketing per se which was illegal, but the "real
message" conveyed by the picketers. As the Court said:

> Thus all of appellants' activities—their powerful trans-
> portation combination, their patrolling, their formation
> of a picket line warning union men not to cross at peril
> of their union membership, their publicizing—constitut-
> ed a single and intregrated course of conduct, which was
> in violation of Missouri's valid law.[14]

Thus, the decision in *Giboney v. Empire Storage & Ice
Co.* stands for little more than the proposition that there

is a "strong governmental interest in certain forms of economic regulation, even though such regulation may have an incidental effect on rights of speech and association."[15]

"Valid State Policy"

The next major decision in the development of picketing theory came in 1957. In *Teamsters, Local 695 v. Vogt, Inc.*,[16] the Teamsters Union set up a picket line outside the entrance of a business, Vogt, Inc. This was because of unsuccessful attempts to unionize Vogt's employees. Vogt suffered economically when suppliers refused to cross the picket lines.

The Supreme Court, in deciding the issue, upheld an injunction banning the picketing. The Court held that the Wisconsin state policy against union coercion was superior to the union's right to picket. (The union was attempting to pressure Vogt to coerce his employees to unionize.)

Justice Felix Frankfurter, author of the decision, held that picketing could be enjoined when it conflicted with a valid state policy "in a domain open to state regulation."[17] Somewhat obscurely Frankfurter declared:

> [T]he Court came to realize that the broad pronouncements, but not the specific holding, of *Thornhill* had to yield "to the impact of facts unforeseen," or at least not sufficiently appreciated. . . . Cases reached the Court in which a State had designed a remedy to meet a specific social policy. These cases made manifest that picketing, even though "peaceful," involved more than just communication of ideas and could not be immune from all state regulation.[18]

This "valid public policy," Frankfurter wrote, could be derived from criminal or civil law and announced by either the legislature or the judiciary, and would permit the issuance of an injunction against even peaceful picketing.[19]

Both Justices William O. Douglas and Hugo Black strenuously dissented (and were joined by Chief Justice Earl Warren). Rather than viewing picketing as conduct per se (and hence always subjugated to any valid state policy), the dissenters urged a close scrutiny of the evil sought to be curbed by the state policy and the specific conduct which supports the unlawful objective.[20] The dissenters objected to the majority's blanket inclusion of all picketing as speech-*plus*, rather than an analysis by way of the "unlawful immediate objective" test as was espoused in *Giboney.* Douglas contended that the activities in *Vogt* amounted to no more than free speech.

The Supreme Court's holding in *Vogt* marked the most repressive era for picketing since *Thornhill.* State courts and legislatures were granted great latitude in regulating peaceful and lawful picketing if there was a valid public policy to justify such restrictions.

The holding in *Vogt,* however, was soon overtaken by a more progressive standard. At any rate, by 1974 in *American Radio Association v. Mobile S. S. Association,*[21] the Supreme Court resolved that *Vogt* was the result of a "growing awareness that these cases involved not so much questions of free speech as review of the balance struck by a State between picketing that involved more than 'publicity' and competing interests of state policy."[22]

Picketing as Freedom of Expression in Its Most Pristine Form

The right to picket was further clarified in 1964 in *NLRB v. Fruit and Vegetable Packers & Warehousemen, Local 760.*[23] This case involved a secondary consumer boycott (a somewhat obscure occurrence which is not necessary to understand for our purposes).[24] The Supreme

Court in upholding the right to picket noted "that a broad ban against peaceful picketing might collide with the guarantees of the First Amendment."[25]

However, it is the concurring opinion of Justice Hugo Black which is of particular interest, since eight years later in *Police Department of City of Chicago v. Mosley*[26] it would be adopted as the Supreme Court's rationale on picketing.[27] According to Justice Black, the decisions regarding picketing did not place picketing outside of state control:

> However, when conduct not constitutionally protected, like patrolling, is intertwined as in picketing, with constitutionally protected free speech and press, regulation of the nonprotected conduct may at the same time encroach on freedom of speech and press. In such cases it is established that it is the duty of courts, before upholding regulations of patrolling, "to weigh the circumstances and to appraise the substantiality of the reasons advanced in support of the regulation of enjoyment of the rights of speech and press."[28]

One year before *NLRB v. Fruit and Vegetable Packers & Warehousemen* was written, however, the next generation of picketing theory cases had their root. The seminal case, *Edwards v. South Carolina*,[29] began a line of antidiscrimination cases which significantly bolstered the right to picket.

8

Antidiscrimination Picketing: Strengthening the Right

Peaceful picketing is the working man's means of communication.

> *Drivers Union v. Meadowmoor Dairies,*
> 312 U.S. 287, 293 (1941)

Freedom to speak and write about public questions is as important to the life of our government as is the heart to the human body. In fact, this privilege is the heart of our Government. If the heart is weakened, the result is debilitation; if it be stilled, the result is death.

> *Milk Wagon Drivers Union v.*
> *Meadowmoor Dairies,*
> 312 U.S. 287, 301 (1941)
> (Black, J., dissenting)

On March 2, 1961, nearly 200 blacks gathered at Zion Baptist Church in Columbia, South Carolina. From there, carrying placards and picket signs, they marched without incident to the State Capitol Building grounds to express their grievances "to the citizens of South Carolina, along with the Legislative Bodies of South Carolina."[1] Justice Potter Stewart described the situation:

As they entered [the Capitol grounds], they were told by the law enforcement officials that "they had a right, as a citizen, to go through the State House grounds, as any other citizen has, as long as they were peaceful." During the next half hour or 45 minutes, the[y] . . . walked single file or two abreast in an orderly way through the grounds, each group carrying placards.[2]

The demonstrators peacefully assembled and expressed their grievances. Not until they were told by police to disband did they do more. As Justice Stewart wrote, "[e]ven then, they but sang patriotic songs after one of their leaders had delivered a 'religious harangue.' There was no violence or threat of violence on their part or on the part of any member of the crowd."[3]

The protestors, because of their refusal to disband, were all charged with a "breach of the peace." The mass arrest of 179 blacks was challenged and upheld by the Supreme Court of South Carolina, even though the offense was, in the words of the court, "not susceptible of exact definition."[4] The United States Supreme Court, in the case of *Edwards v. South Carolina*,[5] asserted that "[t]he circumstances in this case reflect an exercise of these basic constitutional rights in their most pristine and classic form."[6] As such, those activities were protected by the First and Fourteenth Amendments against invasion by the states.

Cox v. Louisiana

Two years after the decision in *Edwards v. South Carolina*, the United States Supreme Court decided *Cox v. Louisiana*.[7] The case involved some leaders of student protestors who were charged with the breach of the peace, obstructing a public passageway,[8] and picketing near a courthouse.[9] The students, while protesting the arrests of twenty-three other students (who had been jailed), remained peaceable. They peaceably assembled at the State Capitol building and marched to the courthouse where they sang, prayed, and listened to a speech.

Carrying picket signs, the protestors sang hymns. The twenty-three students in jail responded by also singing. This was greeted with cheers and applause by the demonstrators.

After a speech by Mr. Cox urging the protestors to "sit-in" at local lunch counters, the police ordered the protestors to disband. The protestors refused, and tear gas was used. Throughout the entire incident the assembly remained peaceable. To this situation the Supreme Court reasserted essential freedoms:

> [A] function of free speech under our system of government is to invite dispute. It may indeed best serve its high purpose when it induces a condition of unrest, creates dissatisfaction with conditions as they are, or even stirs people to anger. Speech is often provocative and challenging. It may strike at prejudices and preconceptions and have profound unsettling effects as it presses for acceptance of an idea. That is why freedom of speech . . . is . . . protected against censorship or punishment. . . . There is no room under our Constitution for a more restrictive view. For the alternative would lead to standardization of ideas either by legislatures, courts, or dominant political or community groups.[10]

As a consequence of this reasoning, the Court reversed Cox's conviction for "breach of the peace," holding the law unconstitutional "in that it sweeps within its broad scope activities that are constitutionally protected free speech and assembly."[11] Cox's conviction for "obstructing a public passageway" was also overturned because, as the Supreme Court noted:

> [T]he practice in Baton Rouge allowing unfettered discretion in local officials in the regulation of the use of the streets for peaceful parades and meetings is an unwarranted abridgment of appellant's freedom of speech and assembly secured to him by the First Amendment, as applied to the States by the Fourteenth Amendment.[12]

The Court also overturned Cox's conviction in the alleged violation of a Louisiana statute in which he was charged with "interfering with . . . the administration of justice . . . [with] pickets or parades in or near a building housing a court of the State of Louisiana."[13] The Supreme Court found that it was not dealing "with the contempt power but with a narrowly drafted statute and not with speech in its pristine form but with conduct of a totally different character."[14] The Court then applied the "clear and present danger" test, albeit hesitantly:

> Even assuming the applicability of a general clear and present danger test . . . crowds, such as this, demonstrating before a courthouse . . . [produce] conduct [which] inherently threatens the judicial process.[15]

The Supreme Court noted that "placards used as an essential and inseparable part of a grave offense against an important public law cannot immunize that unlawful conduct from state control."[16]

Despite this *dicta*, the Supreme Court found in Cox's favor, concluding:

> Liberty can only be exercised in a system of law which safeguards order. We affirm the repeated holding of the Court that our constitutional command of free speech and assembly is basic and fundamental and encompasses peaceful social protest, so important to the preservation of the freedoms treasured in a democratic society. We also reaffirm the repeated decisions of this Court that there is no place for violence in a democratic society dedicated to liberty under law, and that the right of peaceful protest does not mean that everyone with opinions or beliefs to express may do so at any time and at any place. . . . [R]egulation of conduct that involves freedom of speech and assembly [may] not . . . be so broad in scope as to stifle First Amendment freedoms, which "need breathing space to survive."[17]

The separate opinion of Justice Hugo Black[18] is also important to our analysis. Black wrote that a statute "regulating *conduct*—patrolling and marching—as distinguished from *speech*, would . . . be constitutional, subject only to the condition that if such a law had the effect of indirectly impinging on freedom of speech, press, or religion, it would be unconstitutional if under the circumstances it appeared that the State's interest in suppressing the conduct was not sufficient to outweigh the individual's interest in engaging in conduct closely involving his First Amendment freedoms."[19]

Thus, although the Court was ambivalent because of the alleged *"unlawful purpose"* involved (that is, disruption of the Court's judicial proceedings), it nonetheless recognized these activities (including picketing) as protected activities.[20]

The Cox Aftermath

Following *Cox* came *Brown v. Louisiana*,[21] another civil rights case involving expressive activities. In *Brown* five blacks were arrested and charged with a "breach of the peace" for engaging in a "sit-in" at a library which maintained racially discriminatory services. The five defendants were peaceable and quiet and in no way interfered with the operations of the public library. They simply refused to leave the segregated public facility.

The United States Supreme Court, in this 1966 decision, found that these activities were insufficient to justify the convictions for a "breach of the peace." In a plurality opinion Justice Abe Fortas (joined by Chief Justice Warren and Justice Douglas) wrote:

> We are here dealing with an aspect of a basic constitutional right—the right under the First and Fourteenth Amendments guaranteeing freedom of speech and assembly, and freedom to petition the Government for a redress of grievances. . . . As this Court has repeatedly

stated, these rights are not confined to verbal expression. They embrace appropriate types of action which certainly include the right in a peaceable and orderly manner to protest by silent and reproachful presence, in a place where the protestant has every right to be, the unconstitutional segregation of public facilities.[22]

Two other justices, William Brennan and Byron White, concurred in the result.

Relying on *Cox v. Louisiana, Cameron v. Johnson*[23] in 1968 dealt with a constitutional challenge to the Mississippi Anti-Picketing Law which prohibited "picketing . . . in such a manner as to obstruct or unreasonably interfere with free ingress or egress to and from any . . . county . . . courthouses."[24] In a 7-2 decision, the United States Supreme Court cited *Cox,* stating "picketing and parading [are] subject to regulation even though intertwined with expression and association,"[25] and found:

> [T]his statute does not prohibit picketing so intertwined unless engaged in a manner which obstructs or unreasonably interferes with ingress or egress to or from the courthouse. Prohibition of conduct which has this effect does not abridge constitutional liberty "since such activity bears no necessary relationship to the freedom to . . . distribute information or opinion."[26]

Accordingly the Supreme Court upheld the statute.

Four years after *Cox v. Louisiana,* the United States Supreme Court in 1969 decided *Gregory v. City of Chicago.*[27] This important case curtailed the use of the "heckler" veto. In theory the Court reversed the convictions of persons who had peaceably marched to the mayor's residence to protest segregation in Chicago's public schools. After a larger and more unruly crowd of bystanders formed, the Chicago police ordered the protestors to disperse. The protestors refused and were arrested for disorderly conduct. This was in spite of the fact that there was no evidence that the protestors themselves were disorderly. The Supreme Court overturned these convictions.

In the same year the United States Supreme Court restated in *Shuttlesworth v. Birmingham* the general principle that "the First and Fourteenth Amendments [do not] afford the same kind of freedom to those who would communicate ideas by conduct such as patrolling, marching, and picketing on streets and highways, as these amendments afford to those who communicate ideas by pure speech."[28] *Shuttlesworth* challenged an Alabama statute which granted unfettered discretion in granting or denying parade permits. The Court held that their decisions have "made clear that picketing and parading may nonetheless constitute methods of expression, entitled to First Amendment protection,"[29] and therefore the Alabama statute was held unconstitutional.

Although from these decisions it appears that a different standard was being applied to labor and non-labor picketing cases, the United States Supreme Court in *Police Department v. Mosley*[30] refuted this idea. Mr. Mosley, protesting alleged racial discrimination in Chicago's public schools, picketed a Chicago high school in violation of an ordinance which prohibited all picketing except "the peaceful picketing of any school involved in a labor dispute." Because the subject matter (whether it is labor or nonlabor picketing) is determinative, the Court in this 1972 case found the ordinance violative of the equal protection clause of the Fourteenth Amendment:

> Of course, the equal protection claim in this case is closely intertwined with First Amendment interests; the Chicago ordinance affects picketing, which is expressive

conduct; moreover, it does so by classifications formulated in terms of the subject of the picketing. . . . Peaceful picketing on the subject of a school's labor-management dispute is permitted, but all other peaceful picketing is prohibited. The operative distinction is the message on a picket sign. But, above all else, the First Amendment means that government has no power to restrict expression because of its message, its ideas, its subject matter, or its content.[31]

The Court determined that "[b]ecause picketing plainly involves expressive conduct within the protection of the First Amendment . . . discrimination among pickets must be tailored to serve a substantial governmental interest."[32] Finding no such interest, the Supreme Court unanimously concurred in finding the ordinance invalid.

Extensions: Carey and Grace

In 1980 the United States Supreme Court decided *Carey u Brown*,[33] embodying the same issue as was faced in *Mosley* but in a different context—residential picketing. In *Carey* the Supreme Court struck down an Illinois home privacy statute which prohibited all picketing (except labor picketing) on the streets and sidewalks of *residential* neighborhoods. Concerning the statute, the Court held: "On its face, the Act accords preferential treatment to the expression of views on one particular subject; information about labor disputes may be freely disseminated, but discussion of all other issues is restricted."[34]

Hence, *Carey* is in no principled way distinguishable from *Mosley,* and as such *Mosley* is the primary precedent cited. The *dicta* in *Carey u Brown* is also worthy of note:

There can be no doubt that in prohibiting peaceful picketing on the public streets and sidewalks in residential neighborhoods, the Illinois statute regulates expressive conduct that falls within the First Amendment preserve.

... Wherever the title of streets and parks may rest, they have immemorially been held in trust for the use of the public and, time out of mind, have been used for purposes of assembly, communicating thoughts between citizens, and discussing public questions. . . . [S]treets, sidewalks, parks, and other similar public places are so historically associated with the exercise of First Amendment rights that access to them for the purpose of exercising such rights cannot constitutionally be denied broadly and absolutely.[35]

Because exclusions were being made upon the basis of the content of the speech involved, the Illinois statute, like the statute in *Mosley*, was invalid as a violation of the equal protection clause of the Fourteenth Amendment.

It is important to notice that the Court in *Carey* created a "new category" of speech:

The central difficulty with this argument is that it forthrightly presupposes that labor picketing is more deserving of First Amendment protection than are public protests over other issues, particularly the important economic, social, and political subjects about which these appellees wish to demonstrate. We reject that proposition. . . . Public issue picketing, "an exercise of . . . basic constitutional rights in their most pristine and classic form" . . . has always rested on the highest rung of the hierarchy of First Amendment values: The maintenance of the opportunity for free political discussion to the end that government may be responsive to the will of the people and that changes may be obtained by lawful means, an opportunity essential to the security of the Republic, is a fundamental principle of our constitutional system.[36]

Thus *Carey v. Brown* somewhat incongruously states that content-based discrimination in picketing is impermissible and yet maintains that "public-issue picketing" is more deserving of constitutional protection than other forms of picketing. This is a position supported by constitutional authority Thomas Emerson. He convincingly argues that nonlabor picketing is more akin to pure expression than labor picketing and thus should be subject to fewer restrictions.[37] Moreover, this principle was reiterated in *NAACP v. Claiborne Hardware*[38] in 1982 by the United States Supreme Court.

The most recent case directly addressing the issue of picketing is *United States v. Grace*.[39] In *Grace*, Thaddeus Zywicki and Mary Grace sought an injunction declaring invalid a federal statute which made it unlawful " 'to parade, stand, or move in procession or assemblages in the Supreme Court Buildings or grounds,' or 'to display therein any flag, banner, or device designed or adapted to bring into public notice any party, organization, or movement.' "[40] Both Zywicki and Grace were prevented from distributing pamphlets and picketing (respectively) upon the sidewalk abutting the United States Supreme Court grounds. (Grace's picket sign was inscribed with the verbatim text of the First Amendment.)

The Supreme Court determined that such activities "are expressive activities involving speech protected by the First Amendment."[41] As such, the Court held that "the government's ability to permissibly restrict expressive conduct is very limited: the government may enforce reasonable time, place, and manner regulations as long as the restrictions are 'content-neutral, are narrowly tailored to serve a significant government interest, and leave open ample alternative channels of communication.' "[42] The Court further stated that "[a]dditional restrictions such as an *absolute* prohibition on a particular type of expression will be upheld only if narrowly drawn to accomplish a compelling governmental interest."[43]

Therefore, it is clear that an *absolute* prohibition of picketing must meet the same "compelling state interest" test as the restrictions on the "preferred" freedom of "pure" speech. Since the right to picket is a substantial freedom, it is afforded the same protection as other liberties.

9

Picketing and Public Property

Traditional public forum property occupies a special position in terms of First Amendment protection and will not lose its historically recognized character for the reason that it abuts government property that has been dedicated to a use other than as a forum for public expression.

United States v. Grace,
461 U.S. _____ , 103 S. Ct.
1702, 1708
(April 20, 1983)

As we have seen, liberty of self-expression is not an absolute freedom. Speech and speech-related conduct cannot be practiced anywhere with impunity. Clearly few of us would appreciate a Ku Klux Klan meeting or a Nazi rally (or both) in our living room.

It is generally accepted that "one of the essential sticks in the bundle of property rights is the right to exclude others."[1] This is true of both private and governmental properties. The Supreme Court has regularly rejected the assertion that people who wish "to propagandize protests or views have a constitutional right to do so whenever and however and wherever they please."[2]

This right to exclude others, or conversely the public's right to access, will depend upon the character of the property at issue. Those places appropriate for self-expression purposes are generally referred to as "First Amendment forums." These forums can easily be broken down into two categories: (1) government First Amendment forums, and (2) privately owned First Amendment forums. These two categories are treated differently.

Government-Owned First Amendment Forums

Governmentally owned property is not necessarily a First Amendment forum. The First Amendment, the United States Supreme Court has held, "does not guarantee access to property simply because it is owned or controlled by the government."[3] Nor does publicly "owned or operated property . . . become a 'public forum' simply because members of the public are permitted to come and go at will."[4] A recent Supreme Court decision, *Perry Educational Association v. Perry Local Educator's Association,*[5] has to some extent clarified which governmental properties are and are not public forums. These categories are: (1) places which by long tradition or government fiat have been devoted to assembly or debate; (2) public property which has been designated as a forum for public communication; and (3) public property reserved for other than communicative purposes.[6]

Traditional First Amendment Forums

First Amendment forums which are designated by tradition or government fiat as such are constitutionally protected. In these areas, which have been devoted to assembly and debate, the rights of the state to limit expressive activity are sharply circumscribed.

The most recent United States Supreme Court decision regarding this type of a forum is *United States v. Grace.*[7] There Mary Grace and Thaddeus Zywicki contested a federal law which made it unlawful "to parade, stand or move in procession or assemblages in the Supreme Court building."[8] Zywicki and Grace were prevented from distributing leaflets and picketing. Grace was stopped from carrying a four foot by two and a half foot sign quoting the First Amendment.

Since these activities were carried on upon the public sidewalk, the Court noted:

Sidewalks, of course, are among those areas of public property that traditionally have been held open to the public for expressive activities and are clearly within those areas of public property that may be considered, generally without further inquiry, to be public forum property.[9]

The Court further concluded that a legislature "may not by its own *ipse dixit* destroy the 'public forum' status of streets and parks which have historically been public forums."[10]

Ownership need not officially rest in federal, state, or municipal government's hands for such property to qualify as a First Amendment forum. The Supreme Court, as early as 1939, in *Hague v. C.I.O.*[11] held:

Wherever the title of streets and parks may rest, they have immemorially been held in trust for the use of public and, time out of mind, have been used for purposes of assembly, communicating thoughts between citizens, and discussing public questions. Such use of the streets and public places has, from ancient times, been a part of the privileges, immunities, rights, and liberties of citizens. The privilege of a citizen of the United States to use the streets and parks for communication of views on national questions may be regulated in the interest of all; it is not absolute, but relative, and must be exercised in subordination to the general comfort and convenience, and in consonance with peace and good order; but it must not, in the guise of regulation, be abridged or denied.[12]

Thus it is quite clear, as the Supreme Court has held, that "streets, sidewalks, parks, and other similar public places are so historically associated with the exercise of First Amendment rights"[13] that the federal, state and local governments cannot foreclose such forums.[14]

In such a forum, any absolute prohibition of free exercise will be upheld *only* if it is "narrowly drawn to accomplish a compelling governmental interest."[15] A compelling state interest encompasses "[o]nly the gravest abuses, endangering paramount interests; accordingly, only these give occasion for permissible limitation."[16] Therefore, except in cases of extreme emergency, "[i]n these quintessential public forums, the government may not prohibit all communicative activity."[17]

However, it must not be forgotten, as the Supreme Court stressed in *Grace:* "The government may enforce reasonable time, place, and manner regulations as long as the restrictions are content-neutral, are narrowly tailored to serve a significant government interest, and leave open ample alternative channels of communication."[18]

Public Property Which the State Has Opened as a First Amendment Forum

This category of property consists of those governmentally owned places which the state has designated as a forum for public communications. Although the state is under no compulsion to create such a forum, the United States Supreme Court has noted that once a state does open an area for expressive conduct, "the Constitution forbids a state to enforce . . . exclusions."[19]

Government agencies may create a "limited purpose public forum" which exists for the exclusive use of certain groups.[20] An example of such a forum appears in *Widmar v. Vincent*,[21] where the Supreme Court required that equal access must be permitted for religious student groups at the University of Missouri at Kansas City. In this case the state-created forum existed exclusively for use by a certain class of groups—student-initiated organizations.

A state-designated forum may limit discussion to certain subjects. For example, in *City of Madison Joint School District v. Wisconsin Public Employment Relations Commission*[22] it was found permissible to limit self-expression to those topics relevant to school board business. These are two examples of *limited purpose forums.*

Although state and local governments are not compelled by the federal Constitution to keep the designated forum open indefinitely, as long as the government facilities are opened the state is bound by the same standards which are applicable in a traditional public forum. Of course, reasonable time, place, and manner regulations are permissible. Again, however, as the Supreme Court has stressed, any exclusions based upon the *content* of the speech or speech-related conduct must be narrowly drawn to effectuate a compelling state interest.[23]

Once the government has designated an area as an appropriate forum for communicative activity and has opened that forum for use by the general public, the state cannot base exclusions upon the *content* of the speech offered. However, a government can create a limited purpose forum, which may restrict usage to certain groups or certain subjects. Even in limited purpose forums, however, these limitations cannot be used as means to justify content-based discrimination against speech. Such an "exclusionary policy violates the fundamental principle that a state regulation of speech should be content-neutral."[24]

Public Property Reserved for Other Than Communicative Purposes

In the grouping of cases decided under this category it is clear that the Supreme Court "recognized that the First Amendment does not guarantee access to property simply because it is owned or controlled by the government."[25] It has also been well established by the Court that "[t]he state, no less than a private owner of property, has power to preserve the property under its control for the use to which it is lawfully dedicated."[26]

The case that formulated these principles was *Adderley v. Florida.*[27] In *Adderley* the United States Supreme Court faced a challenge to the arrest and conviction of thirty-one student demonstrators who entered jailhouse grounds to protest racial segregation. The county sheriff (the legal custodian of the jail and jail grounds) asked the students to leave the grounds. Their refusal led to their arrest.

The areas where the students congregated were a "jail entrance and driveway [which] were not normally used by the public, but by the sheriff's department for transporting prisoners to and from the courts several blocks away and by commercial concerns for servicing the jailed."[28] Thus the protest interfered with the function to which that property was dedicated, as well as blocked all routes of ingress and egress to vehicular traffic.[29] To the Court, the following was particularly determinative:

> There is not a shred of evidence in this record that this power was exercised, or that its exercise was sanctioned by the lower courts, because the sheriff objected to what was being said by the demonstrators or because he disagreed with the objective of their protest. The record reveals that he objected only to their presence on that part of the jail grounds reserved for jail purposes.[30]

The Supreme Court upheld the convictions, since there was no impermissible content-based discrimination evidenced.

In a 1974 case, *Lehman v. City of Shaker Heights*,[31] the United States Supreme Court upheld the refusal by a city transit company to rent space on its vehicles for partisan political advertising. Under the policy, commercial advertising was acceptable, whereas political advertising was banned. It was feared that permitting political advertisements would jeopardize long-term commercial advertising revenue, subject commuters to political propaganda, and lead to political favoritism.[32] Because of this, the Court later recounted that the holding in *Lehman* "concluded that partisan political speech would disrupt the operation of governmental facilities even though other forms of speech posed no such danger."[33]

Similarly, in the 1976 decision in *Greer v. Spock*[34] the Supreme Court held that the federal government could prohibit partisan political speech on a military base (Fort Dix) even though civilian speakers had been allowed to lecture on other topics. Once again the justification for such a prohibition was the avoidance of disruption to those activities that the facilities were created to serve.

In *United States Postal Service v. Greenburgh Civic Association*,[35] analogous reasoning was used by the Supreme Court in 1981 to uphold Congressional restrictions upon unpaid access to the mail system. Greenburgh Civil Association challenged the legislation as a violation of freedom of speech (assuming that the mailboxes are First Amendment forums). The Court found that it was essential to the fiscal integrity of the postal system that mail revenues be protected and efficient delivery of the mails be facilitated. Thus handbills and pamphlets could not be privately deposited into post boxes. Mailboxes are not a First Amendment forum, but rather a public property reserved for other purposes.[36]

Therefore, "the state may reserve the forum for its intended purposes, communicative or otherwise, as long as the regulation on speech is reasonable and not an effort to suppress expression merely because public officials oppose the speaker's view."[37] In addition, as previously noted, reasonable time, place, and manner restrictions may be placed upon communicative activities.

10

Picketing and Private Property

Ownership does not mean absolute dominion. The more an owner, for his advantage, opens up his property for use by the public in general, the more his property rights become circumscribed by the statutory and constitutional rights of those who use it.

Marsh v. Alabama,
326 U.S. 501, 506 (1946)

One of the "sticks" in the bundle of property rights is the power to exclude others from one's property. As a general rule, for private personal ownership this right is nearly absolute. However, in certain instances where a privately owned facility or property is held out for general public use, the right to exclude others becomes more sharply curtailed.

Private Property Rights and Freedom of Expression
The seminal United States Supreme Court case establishing the idea of a "quasi-public" facility was decided in 1946 in *Marsh v. Alabama.*[1] Chickasaw, a suburb of Mobile, Alabama, was owned entirely by Gulf Shipbuilding Corporation. The corporation performed many of the services traditionally performed by municipal governments. As the Court described the situation:

The property consists of residential buildings, streets, a system of sewers, a sewage disposal plant and a "business block" on which business places are situated. . . . [T]he residents use the business block as their regular shopping center. To do so, they now, as they have for many years, make use of a company-owned paved street and sidewalk located alongside the store fronts in order to enter and leave the stores and the post office. Intersecting company-owned roads at each end of the business block lead into a four-lane public highway which runs parallel to the business block at a distance of thirty feet. There is nothing to stop highway traffic from coming onto the business block and upon arrival a traveler may make free use of the facilities available there. In short the town and its shopping district are accessible to and freely used by the public.[2]

Grace Marsh, a Jehovah's Witness, attempted to distribute pamphlets and to proselytize outside a United States Post Office in Chickasaw. Town officials warned Marsh to leave Chickasaw. However, she refused and was arrested for violation of Alabama's criminal trespass law. Her defense, predicated upon freedom of press and religion as guaranteed by the First Amendment, proved to be unsuccessful in the Alabama courts.

In *Marsh v. Alabama* the United States Supreme Court reversed the earlier decision, explaining that under the facts, the First Amendment protections outweighed private property rights:

Ownership does not always mean absolute dominion. The more an owner, for his advantage, opens up his property for use by the public in general, the more do his rights become circumscribed by the statutory and constitutional rights of those who use it. . . . *Since these facilities are built and operated primarily to benefit the public and since their operation is essentially a public function, it is subject to state regulation.*[3]

In deciding that Grace Marsh had the right to distribute the religious literature, and, equally important, the residents of the town had a right to receive communication freely, the Court said:

> The managers appointed by the corporation cannot curtail the liberty of press and religion of these people consistently with purposes of the constitutional guarantees, and a state statute, as the one here involved, which enforces such action by criminally punishing those who attempt to distribute religious literature clearly violates the First and Fourteenth Amendments to the Constitution.[4]

As a later case explained *Marsh*, central in this determination (that the streets of Chickasaw were a First Amendment forum) were two factors:

> *Marsh v. Alabama* . . . involved the assumption by a private enterprise of all the attributes of a state-created municipality and the exercise by that enterprise of semiofficial municipal functions as a delegate of the State. In effect, the owner of the company town was performing the full spectrum of municipal powers and stood in the shoes of the State.[5]

This is commonly referred to as the "public function" doctrine. It is composed of two basic elements. First, the private enterprise must possess all of the *attributes* of a municipality. Second, the private enterprise must exercise semiofficial municipal functions. As the Supreme Court noted, Chickasaw, Alabama, except for the fact that title to the property "is owned by the Gulf Shipbuilding Corporation . . . has all the characteristics of any other American town. The property consists of residential buildings, streets, a system of sewers, a sewage disposal plant and a 'business block' on which business places are situated."[6]

Therefore, the Supreme Court, after balancing the constitutional proprietary rights of the owners against the preferred freedoms of press, religion, and speech, reversed Marsh's conviction for trespassing. The private-property interests of a "company town" could not justify infringment of free speech.

Logan Valley Plaza

Twenty-two years later the United States Supreme Court extended the *Marsh* reasoning in deciding *Amalgamated Food v. Logan Valley Plaza.*[7]

In *Logan Valley* a Pennsylvania state court enjoined picketing of a supermarket in a *privately owned* shopping center. The store and the Logan Valley Plaza owned the parking area which served the entire shopping center. Public highways were between 350 to 500 feet from the supermarket.

Nonunion employees worked in the market, and the Amalgated Food Employees Union began picketing with the purpose of forcing the food store to employ union workers. Picketing was carried on in the pickup lane in front of the market and at the porch of the building.

The property owners sought and obtained an injunction which prohibited all picketing on private property as a violation of the trespass laws of the state of Pennsylvania. Thereafter the union continued picketing adjacent to the public highways, but sought dissolution of the injunction. The union contested the injunction, believing the trespass laws as applied violated their First and Fourteenth Amendment "right to picket."

On appeal, the Supreme Court held that Logan Valley Plaza was "the functional equivalent of the business district of Chickasaw involved in *Marsh.*"[8] This reasoning was based upon the invitation to the general public to do business on the property. As a consequence, property rights were subjugated to the First Amendment picketing rights. And with respect to use of the trespass laws, the Court in *Logan* held:

> [T]he State may not delegate the power, through the use of its trespass laws, wholly to exclude those members of the public wishing to exercise their First Amendment rights on the premises in a manner and for a purpose generally consonant with the use to which the property is actually put.[9]

Justice Hugo Black, the author of the *Marsh* opinion, wrote a vigorous dissent. He argued that the exception carved out in *Marsh* was intended to include a company town which took on *all* the attributes of a municipality and such an exception should not be extended to a shopping center solely on the business district factor.[10]

Lloyd Corporation v. Tanner

Logan Valley Plaza reserved the question of whether property rights could, consistent with the First Amendment, prevent picketing when the purpose was unrelated to the use to which the business property was being put. That question came before the United States Supreme Court in 1972 in *Lloyd Corporation v. Tanner*.[11]

Lloyd Corporation owned a shopping mall that took in fifty acres, twenty of which served as parking area around it. Public streets and sidewalks ran through the property at various locations but not into the mall itself.

On November 14, 1968, Mr. Tanner and four other young people entered the Lloyd Center and began handing out leaflets inviting the public to a meeting of the "Resistance Community" to protest United States involvement in the Vietnam War. The mall prohibited all forms of handbilling. Security guards informed those engaged in the distribution that they would either stop or be arrested for trespassing. They did cease the hand-billing, but brought a legal action to declare the Lloyd Center to be an open forum for their activity.

The lower court followed the *Marsh-Logan Valley Plaza* line of cases in allowing such activity on private property. However, the United States Supreme Court restricted *Logan Valley Plaza* by holding that the privately owned sidewalks and streets of a business district are not the equivalent of municipal sidewalks and streets for First Amendment purposes.

Two elements were distinctive under the *Logan* decision which were not present in *Lloyd Corporation*. As the Court noted, the picketing in *Logan Valley Plaza* was "directly related in its purpose to the use to which the shopping center property was being put . . . and where the store was located in the center of a large private enclave with the consequence that *no other reasonable opportunities for the pickets to convey their message* to their intended audience were available."[12]

The handbilling protest of the Vietnam War was, of course, totally *un*related to any of the business activities carried on in the mall. Therefore, as the Court explained, the invitation to shop therein was not an invitation to use the mall for any and all purposes. Furthermore, the public sidewalks and roads that ran through the Lloyd site gave an adequate alternative to carry on the handbilling without infringing the property rights of the Lloyd Corporation.

Lloyd Corporation, then, vindicated property rights over First Amendment rights *under the facts of the case.* As Justice Lewis Powell, writing for the majority, stated:

> In terms of being open to the public, there are differences only of degree—not of principle—between a free-standing store and one located in a shopping center, between a small store and a large one, between a single

store with some malls and open areas designed to attract customers and Lloyd Center with its elaborate malls and interior landscaping.[13]

The opinion in *Lloyd Corporation* did not state that *Logan Valley Plaza* was overruled, although *Lloyd Corporation* can be seen as limiting the *Logan Valley Plaza* holding. However, in 1976 in *Hudgens v. N.L.R.B.*[14] the Supreme Court was once again confronted with facts similar to those of *Logan Valley Plaza*. Warehouse employees of Butler Shoe Company went on strike and picketed a Butler retail store inside a shopping mall. The privately owned shopping center was surrounded by a large parking lot and housed sixty businesses. Management of the mall threatened those engaged in the picketing with arrest for criminal trespass if they did not leave. The union subsequently filed an unfair labor practice complaint with the National Labor Relations Board.

Ultimately the case reached the Supreme Court only to be remanded to the Board for a decision to be made exclusively under the National Labor Relations Act (rather than partially on the rationale of *Lloyd Corporation*).

A new approach was articulated by the Supreme Court in *Hudgens*. The Court first repeated that the First and Fourteenth Amendments prevented only government from abridgment of free speech, not owners of private property. Going further, however, the decision concluded that guarantees of *free speech had no part to play in a case of this type.* Moreover, even when it could be said that private property had taken on the functional equivalent of a municipality, it was not within the government's power to regulate the content of speech.

The Supreme Court in *Hudgens* found that "the rationale of *Logan Valley* did not survive the Court's decision in the *Lloyd* case. . . . [T]he ultimate holding in *Lloyd* amounted to a total rejection of the holding in *Logan Valley*."[15] Hence, *Logan Valley Plaza* was effectively overruled. Justice Powell concurred and Chief Justice Warren Burger joined, stating: "I now agree with Mr. Justice Black, that the opinions in these cases cannot be harmonized in a principled way. Upon more mature thought, I have concluded that we would have been wiser in *Lloyd Corp.* to have confronted this disharmony rather than draw distinctions based upon rather attenuated factual differences."[16] Thus, the author of *Lloyd Corporation v. Tanner* recanted of his decision.

Pruneyard Shopping Center
Pruneyard Shopping Center v. Robins,[17] decided by the Supreme Court in 1980, is the latest decision respecting the extent to which activities may lawfully be exercised on private property.

Factually *Pruneyard Shopping Center* is similar to *Lloyd Corporation* in that a small group of high school students entered the common area of the shopping center to distribute pamphlets to solicit support in opposition to the United Nations resolution against "Zionism." A security guard ordered the protestors to leave, which they did. Later, however, the students brought a legal action to gain access to the Pruneyard Shopping Center.

The California Supreme Court held "that the California Constitution protects 'speech and petitioning, reasonably exercised, in shopping centers even when the centers are privately owned.' "[18]

The United States Supreme Court upheld the decision. The distinction between *Lloyd Corporation* and *Pruneyard Shopping Center* is that while a shopping center owner does not create a First Amendment forum (via the "public function" doctrine) by opening up a shopping mall to the general public, a state constitution or a state by exercising its police power may grant more extensive expressive rights than are secured under the federal Constitution. The United States Supreme Court noted:

> Our reasoning in *Lloyd*, however, does not *ex proprio vigore* limit the authority of the State to exercise its police power or its sovereign right to adopt in its own Constitution individual liberties more expansive than those conferred by the Federal Constitution.[19]

Justice Powell, in concurring, wrote:

> Significantly different questions would be presented if a State authorized strangers to picket or distribute leaflets in privately owned, freestanding stores and commercial premises. Nor does our decision today apply to all "shopping centers."[20]

Powell also addressed the property owner's right of free speech and the right not to be forced to speak to redress views of various groups that may select his or her property as their particular forum:

> A property owner also may be faced with speakers who wish to use his premises as a platform for views that he finds morally repugnant. Numerous examples come to mind. A minority-owned business confronted with leaflet distributors from the American Nazi Party or the Ku Klux Klan, a church-operated enterprise asked to host demonstrations in favor of abortion, or a union compelled to supply a forum to right-to-work advocates could be placed in an intolerable position if state law requires it to make its private property available to anyone who wishes to speak. The strong emotions evoked by speech in such situations may virtually compel the proprietor to respond.[21]

Thus, as the present case law stands, the extent of constitutional protection granted to freedom of speech on private property will, in many instances, be determined by state laws and constitutions rather than the federal Bill of Rights.[22]

11

State Laws Concerning Picketing

> [G]overnment may not grant the use of a forum to people whose views it finds acceptable, but deny use to those wishing to express less favored or more controversial views. And it may not select which issues are worth discussing or debating. . . . [G]overnment may not prohibit others from assembling or speaking on the basis of what they intend to say.
>
> *Police Department of Chicago v. Mosley,*
> 408 U.S. 92, 96 (1972)

The fact that pamphleteering, picketing, and sidewalk counseling are expressive activities involving constitutionally protected "speech" does not end the inquiry. These activities, as has been noted, must be exercised within the parameters of a First Amendment forum. Beyond this, certain other state laws and regulations may be valid. Others may not be.

Absolute Prohibition

It was clearly established in 1983 in *United States v. Grace*[1] that in the picketing and pamphleteering contexts, "an *absolute* prohibition on a particular type of expression will be upheld only if narrowly drawn to accomplish a *compelling governmental interest.*"[2] And, as the United States Supreme Court held in *Carey v. Brown:*[3]

> [S]treets, sidewalks, parks, and other similar public places are so historically associated with the exercise of First Amendment rights that access to them for the purpose of exercising such rights *cannot constitutionally be denied broadly and absolutely.*[4]

Therefore, except under exigent circumstances, peaceful picketing, pamphleteering, and sidewalk counseling cannot be abridged.

Content Censorship

In *Police Department of Chicago v. Mosley*[5] the Supreme Court reviewed a Chicago ordinance which prohibited picketing next to a school (although an exemption was made for peaceful labor picketing). The Court found:

> The central problem with Chicago's ordinance is that it describes permissible picketing in terms of its subject matter. Peaceful picketing on the subject of a school's labor-management dispute is permitted, but all other peaceful picketing is prohibited. The operative distinction is the message on a picket sign. But, above all else, the First Amendment means that government has no power to restrict expression because of its message, its ideas, its subject matter, or its content. . . . To permit the continued building of our politics and culture, and to assure self-fulfillment for each individual, our people are guaranteed the right to express any thought, free from government censorship. The essence of this forbidden censorship is content control.[6]

The Supreme Court in *Mosley* adopts a strong anti-censorship stance:

> [T]rying to prescribe by law what matters of public interest people whom it allows to assemble on its streets may and may not discuss . . . [is] censorship in a most odious form.[7]

The Court found the Chicago ordinance in violation of both the First Amendment and the equal protection clause of the Fourteenth Amendment. Finally, the Supreme Court in *United States v. Grace*[8] draws the bottom line:

> [T]he government's ability to permissibly restrict expressive conduct is very limited: the government may enforce reasonable time, place, and manner regulations as long as the restrictions "are content-neutral, are narrowly tailored to serve a significant government interest, and leave open ample alternative channels of communication."[9]

Prior Restraints

Prior restraints (hindering or prohibiting speech before it occurs) upon the freedom of expression come in two forms: administrative preclearances and injunctions. *Shuttlesworth v. City of Birmingham*[10] discusses the first of these:

> [W]e have consistently condemned licensing systems which vest in an administrative official discretion to grant or withhold a permit upon broad criteria unrelated to proper regulation of public places. . . . Even when the use of its public streets and sidewalks is involved, therefore, a municipality may not empower its licensing officials to roam essentially at will, dispensing or withholding permission to speak, assemble, picket, or parade, according to their own opinions regarding the potential effect of the activity in question on the "welfare," "decency," or "morals" of the community."[11]

The United States Supreme Court in 1951 in *Niemotko v. Maryland*[12] reiterated earlier holdings in this regard:

> In those [earlier] cases this Court condemned statutes and ordinances which required that permits be obtained

from local officials as a prerequisite to the use of public places, on the grounds that a license requirement constitutes a prior restraint on freedom of speech, press and religion, and in the absence of narrowly drawn, reasonable and definite standards for officials to follow, must be invalid.[13]

Thus, "narrow, objective, and definite standards to guide the licensing authority"[14] are a prerequisite for constitutional validity.

The second form of a prior restraint is the use of an injunction. Contempt charges for violating an injunction under a constitutionally infirm statute were upheld in *Walker v. Birmingham.*[15] Justice Potter Stewart, writing for the Supreme Court, noted that "respect for judicial process is a small price to pay for the civilizing hand of the law."[16] In *Walker* the Court acknowledged that it would be a different situation if an injunction were "transparently invalid."[17]

Thus, patently unconstitutional injunctions fall under a kind of "plain error" rule and may be challenged by disobedience, while latently unconstitutional injunctions could not be.[18] As the Supreme Court has held in various cases: "Any prior restraint on expression comes to th[e] [Supreme] Court with a 'heavy presumption' against its constitutional validity."[19]

Overbreadth and Vagueness

Regulations which "sweep within its broad scope activities that are constitutionally protected speech and assembly"[20] are termed "overbroad." Therefore, as the Supreme Court has held:

> The crucial question, then, is whether the ordinance sweeps within its prohibitions what may not be punished under the First and Fourteenth Amendments.[21]

If the restrictions do sweep in constitutionally protected activity, they are constitutionally invalid and should be challenged.

An example of a valid regulation occurred in the facts surrounding the Supreme Court's decision in *Cameron v. Johnson*.[22] Because the statute in *Cameron* only restricted picketing which blocked ingress and egress, it was sufficiently narrow to escape "overbreadth" infirmity.

Vagueness is that attribute in a restriction which makes it "so vague that men of common intelligence must necessarily guess at its meaning and differ as to its application."[23] Either one of these faults can result in the invalidation of speech restrictive legislation. The United States Supreme Court in *Cox v. Louisiana*[24] has recognized:

> Maintenance of the opportunity for free political discussion is a basic tenet of our constitutional democracy. As Chief Justice Hughes stated in *Stromberg v. California*, 283 U.S. 359, 369 . . . "A statute which upon its face, and as authoritatively construed, is so vague and indefinite as to permit the punishment of the fair use of this opportunity is repugnant to the guaranty of liberty contained in the Fourteenth Amendment."[25]

Time, Place, and Manner
In *United States v. Grace*[26] the United States Supreme Court reaffirmed that the government may enforce reasonable time, place, and manner regulations as long as the restrictions "are content-neutral, are narrowly tailored to serve a significant government interest, and leave open ample alternative channels of communication."[27] Moreover, as the Court has noted:

> [T]he essence of time, place, or manner regulation lies in the recognition that various methods of speech, regard-

less of their content, may frustrate legitimate governmental goals.[28]

In determining whether certain time, place, and manner regulations are valid, the Supreme Court has held that "[t]he nature of a place, 'the pattern of its normal activities, dictate the kinds of regulations of time, place, and manner that are reasonable.' . . . *The crucial question is whether the manner of expression is basically incompatible with the normal activity of a particular place at a particular time.* Our cases make clear that in assessing the reasonableness of regulation, we must weigh heavily the fact that communication is involved."[29]

Examples of time, place, and manner restrictions were set forth by the Supreme Court as early as 1940:

> For example, a person could not exercise this liberty by taking his stand in the middle of a crowded street, contrary to traffic regulations, and maintain his position to the stoppage of all traffic; a group of distributors could not insist upon a constitutional right to form a cordon across the street and to allow no pedestrian to pass who did not accept a tendered leaflet; nor does the guarantee of freedom of speech or of the press deprive a municipality of power to enact regulations against throwing literature broadcast in the streets.[30]

Other examples of reasonable time, place, and manner regulations include efforts "to prevent confusion by overlapping parades or processions, to secure convenient use of the streets by other travelers, and to minimize the risk of disorder."[31]

Manner restrictions may also be applied by governing bodies. For example, the numbers of demonstrators may be limited[32] and their mischievous activities curtailed.[33] Examples of improper manners of expression are obvious. As the Supreme Court has held: "No matter what its message, a roving sound truck that blares at 2 A.M. disturbs neighborhood tranquility"[34] and, as such, may be restricted.

Time, place, and manner requirements, however, must also permit "ample alternative channels for communications."[35] Because these ample alternative channels of communications must remain open, the Supreme Court has held on more than one occasion that "one is not to have the exercise of his liberty of expression in appropriate places abridged on the plea that it may be exercised in some other place."[36]

Caveat: Tortious Interference with Business or Contractual Relations and the Right to Privacy

Even though one may be exercising what he or she believes to be a constitutional right to public discourse or to picket a particular establishment, there is the possibility in any given situation that the person involved could be charged with (1) tortious interference with business or contractual relationships, or (2) the violation of the right to privacy.* It is emphasized, therefore, that before engaging in any type of activity that could possibly result in such a situation, one should seek advice from a competent attorney or attorneys.

Most states recognize a legal cause of action for which damages may be recovered in a court of law for improper interference with both existing contractual relations and prospective contractual relationships. Variations as to the necessary elements in recovering damages for such a tortious interference abound.

For example, as to intentional interference with contractual relations, a federal district court in 1983

---

*The Rutherford Institute has prepared a detailed legal memorandum covering tortious interference and the right to privacy. For information on this memorandum, write to Box 510, Manassas, Virginia 22110.

listed the necessary elements of the tort: (1) the existence of a valid contract between the plaintiff and third parties; (2) knowledge by the defendant of the contract; (3) intent by the defendant to induce or cause the third party not to perform; (4) actions by the defendant which induce or cause nonperformance of the contract; and, (5) resulting damage to the plaintiff.[37]

Available defenses against a suit for tortious interference seem to fall into three broad categories. These are: (1) interference arising from the exercise of an absolute right; (2) interference deriving from the need to protect a third party; and (3) interference in inhering in issues protective of the public interest.

Within these categories one can invoke the First Amendment right to speak freely on controversial issues. A 1978 federal court of appeals decision, *Feminist Women's Health Center, Inc. v. Mohammed*,[38] specifically considered the First Amendment right of free speech as against tortious interference with business or contractual relations. Doctors who had formerly performed abortions at the clinic were allegedly interfering with the clinic's business relations with its present doctors. The former doctors had disagreements with the clinic concerning advertising and aftercare of patients.

The court in *Mohammed* found that the activity of petitioning the government (a complaint letter to the Florida Board of Medical Examiners) was protected against liability for this tort. The court, however, declined comment as to whether other activities were so protected. These other activities included: (1) a letter to the head of the residency program at Jacksonville Hospital; (2) communications to the Capitol Medical Society (presumably a private organization) regarding the Center's abortion clinic; and (3) certain discussions among staff members of Tallahassee Memorial and Jacksonville Hospital regarding their members' medical practice.

Moreover, the court left open the question as to whether the defendants' "alleged concern for the public welfare" would constitute adequate justification or excuse under state law; but it hinted that mere persuasion, rather than threats, might be acceptable to shield them from liability (adding that the issue of justification or excuse is a complex one to be decided by weighing numerous factors).[39]

The right to privacy may also be implicated in situations concerning public discourse and picketing. One court has held that there are actually four distinct torts contemplated under rubric "invasion of privacy" to which danger may accrue: (1) intrusion into one's solitude or into his private affairs; (2) placing an individual in a false light; (3) appropriating an individual's name or likeness for the advantage of another; and (4) the public disclosure of private facts.[40]

Although there might be a state law which provides damages for invasion of privacy, it may be overridden by the First Amendment right of free expression. The United States Supreme Court, for example, in the 1975 decision of *Erznoznik v. City of Jacksonville*,[41] summarized prior decisions of the Court on this subject. Most cases involved the government's attempt to preserve the public's right to privacy from the speech of others. The Court, in *Erznoznik*, reaffirmed that the government must demonstrate that substantial privacy interests are being invaded in an essentially intolerable manner before it may terminate discourse solely to protect others from hearing it.[42]

Conclusion

Freedom of discussion, if it would fulfill its historic function in this nation, must embrace all issues about which information is needed or appropriate to enable the members of society to cope with the exigencies of their period.

Thornhill u Alabama,
310 U.S. 88, 102 (1940)

12

If You Can Keep It

A page of history is worth a volume of logic.
　　　Supreme Court Justice Oliver Wendell Holmes, Jr.

As the delegates of the Constitutional Convention trudged out of Independence Hall on September 17, 1787, an anxious woman in the crowd waiting at the entrance inquired of Benjamin Franklin, "Well, Doctor, what have we got, a republic or a monarchy?" Legend has it that Franklin replied, "A republic, if you can keep it."

Therein lies a central principle of this book—that is, freedom will prevail only if *we* keep open the marketplace of ideas. This means that the people must be ever vigilant in protecting their liberties. This is the way we can keep our republic.

A Page of History
Oliver Wendell Holmes is, indeed, correct in asserting: "A page of history is worth a volume of logic." Those who are unwilling to learn from history will inevitably repeat its past failures.

The present world is increasingly composed of tyrannical statutes which deny the right to speak freely and imprison those who dare speak their mind. In fact, the growth and power of such states is, as some argue, the most significant political development of the twentieth century.[1]

Former presidential adviser Bertram Gross has detailed the growth of the modern state.[2] For example, by 1950 what has commonly been called the "free world" had shrunk from over 90 to less than 70 percent of the world's population. By the year 2000—if the current trend continues—the ratio between free and oppressive governments may well shrink from 65:35 to 50:50. As Gross points out, the implications from such a shift are enormous.[3]

Unfortunately the past is repeating itself worldwide. The ghosts of Adolf Hitler and Joseph Stalin seem to stalk the corridors of the earth.

This places a special burden on the present generation of free societies to keep the freedom we have and to restore it where freedom has been lost. At the same time we must be careful not to repeat the historical mistake in following pied pipers of either the left or right who seek repressive measures to silence those with whom they disagree.

Those who won our independence believed that the greatest menace to freedom is an inert people. The framers of our founding documents knew that public discussion and debate is a public duty incumbent upon *all* citizens. This should always remain a fundamental principle in the American government. And we should always eschew silence coerced by the law.

The Chains of Freedom

Throughout our history we have frequently overcome tendencies toward apathy and political inertia. Thanks to the wisdom of those who armed us with the Constitution, we have thwarted attempts to destroy freedom through coercive law.

This, of course, means standing when standing is

difficult. It means speaking when silence is commanded. It means holding the authorities to the black letter of the law and not allowing officials to distort by way of "interpretation" our most sacred rights. In the words of Thomas Jefferson: "Our peculiar security is in the possession of a written Constitution. Let us not make it a blank paper by construction."[4]

Unfortunately there are ever increasing efforts to thwart freedom in this country. These attacks seem to mount in strength and subtlety. They can be abetted only by our success in implanting in the coming generation respect, tolerance, and compassion for all human beings. This will include an appreciation of the Constitution and its history and the intelligent and independent concern of those who enjoy it.

Finally, I would pray that the concerns expressed here would become part of the American fabric. It is essential that we work together to bring to public notice the simple remedies that will, as the Declaration of Independence proclaims, "secure the blessings of liberty to ourselves and our posterity."

Notes

Introduction
1. Abe Fortas, *Concerning Dissent and Civil Disobedience* 24 (New York: Signet, 1968).
2. *Cox v New Hampshire,* 312 U.S. 569, 574 (1941).

Chapter 1: Truth in the Marketplace
1. John Milton, *Areopagitica, A Speech for the Liberty of Unlicensed Printing to the Parliament of England* (1644), as reproduced in Norman Dorsen, Paul Bender, and Burt Neuborne, eds., 1 *Emerson, Haber and Dorsen's Political and Civil Rights in the United States* (Boston, Mass.: Little, Brown, 1976), p. 3.
2. 250 U.S. 616, 624 (1919) (Holmes, J., dissenting).
3. *Kovacs v Cooper,* 336 U.S. 77 (1949).
4. *Id.* at 95 (Frankfurter, J., concurring).
5. *Roth v United States,* 354 U.S. 476, 484 (1957).
6. *Red Lion Broadcasting Co. v FCC,* 395 U.S. 367, 386 (1969).
7. *Garrison v Louisiana,* 379 U.S. 64, 74-75 (1964).
8. *Carey v Brown,* 447 U.S. 455, 467 (1980).
9. *NAACP v Claiborne Hardware,* 458 U.S. 886, 913 (1982). *See also New York Times v Sullivan,* 376 U.S. 254, 270 (1964).

Chapter 2: The Freedoms of Religion, Speech, and Assembly
1. *Stanley v Georgia,* 394 U.S. 557, 564 (1969), citing *Olmstead v United States,* 277 U.S. 438, 478 (1928) (Brandeis, J., dissenting).
2. 310 U.S. 269 (1940).
3. *Id.* at 303-304.
4. *Id.* at 308-309.
5. *Id.* at 307.
6. *Id.* at 308 and 311.
7. *Id.* at 304.
8. It is interesting to note that in *Prince v Massachusetts,* 321 U.S. 158, 164 (1944), and in *Widmar v Vincent,* 454 U.S. 263, 273, n. 13 (1981), the Court expresses the view that the freedom of religion guarantees and the freedom of speech guarantees are

not synonymous. In *Prince*, no greater liberty was granted by the free exercise clause to religiously motivated speech than was afforded by the free speech provision of the First Amendment.

9. *Thomas v. Review Board*, 450 U.S. 707, 713-716 (1981); *Wisconsin v. Yoder*, 406 U.S. 205, 215-217 (1972).

10. *Wisconsin v. Yoder*, 406 U.S. 205, 215-216 (1972); *Sherbert v. Verner*, 374 U.S. 398, 403 (1963).

11. See *Sherbert v. Verner*, 374 U.S. 398, 403 (1963). A "compelling state interest," which creates an "occasion for permissible limitation" of religious activity, is itself ideally responsive to "only the gravest abuses, endangering paramount interests. . . ." *Thomas v. Collins*, 323 U.S. 516, 530 (1945). Cf. *Sherbert v. Verner*, 374 U.S. 398, 408 (1963).

12. *Sherbert v. Verner*, 374 U.S. 398, 407 (1963).

13. 249 U.S. 47 (1919).

14. *Id.* at 52.

15. *Id.* (emphasis supplied).

16. For a full discussion of the "clear and present danger" test *see Brandenburg v. Ohio*, 395 U.S. 444, 450 (1969) (Douglas, J., concurring). *Also see* McKay, *The Preference For Freedom*, 34 N.Y.U.L. Rev. 1182, 1203-1212 (1959).

17. *Consolidated Edison Co. v. Public Service Commission*, 447 U.S. 530, 540 (1979); *First National Bank of Boston v. Bellotti*, 435 U.S. 765, 786 (1978).

18. These include: fighting words—*Chaplinsky v. New Hampshire*, 315 U.S. 568 (1942); obscenity—*Roth v. United States*, 354 U.S. 476 (1957), and *Miller v. California*, 413 U.S. 15 (1973); libel—*Gertz v. Robert Welch, Inc.*, 418 U.S. 323 (1974), and *Time, Inc. v. Firestone*, 424 U.S. 448 (1976); and incitement—*Brandenburg v. Ohio*, 395 U.S. 444 (1969).

19. *Organization for a Better Austin v. Keefe*, 402 U.S. 415, 419 (1971).

20. *NAACP v. Claiborne Hardware*, 458 U.S. 886, 927 (1982). *Cf. Chaplinsky v. New Hampshire*, 315 U.S. 568, 572 (1942).

21. *Schenck v. United States*, 249 U.S. 47, 52 (1919).

22. *Chaplinsky v. New Hampshire*, 315 U.S. 568, 572, 573 (1942). "The word 'offensive' is not to be defined in terms of what a particular addressee thinks. . . . The test is what men of common intelligence would understand would be words likely to cause an average addressee to fight. . . . The English language has a number of words and expressions which by general consent are 'fighting words' when said without a disarming smile. . . . Such words, as ordinary men know, are likely to cause a fight. So are threatening, profane or obscene revilings." *Coate v. Cincinnati*, 402 U.S. 611, 613, n. 3 (1971).

23. 315 U.S. 568 (1942).

24. 337 U.S. 1 (1949).

25. *Id.* at 4.

26. *Cf. Cohen v. California*, 403 U.S. 15 (1971); *Gooding v. Wilson*, 405 U.S. 518 (1972); and *Lewis v. City of New Orleans*, 415 U.S. 130 (1974).

27. *Organization for a Better Austin v. Keefe*, 402 U.S. 415, 419 (1971). *See also Hess v. California*, 414 U.S. 105, 107 (1973). (The statement " 'We'll take the [expletive deleted] street later.' held not obscene"); *Cohen v. California*, 403 U.S. 15, 25 (1971). (Similar language in disparagement of the draft caused the Court to find that "matters of personal taste" in such usage of language were not obscene.)

28. *NAACP v. Claiborne Hardware*, 458 U.S. 886, 911, n. 46 (1982); *Watts v. United States*, 394 U.S. 705, 708 (1969). *See also*, Farber, *Commercial Speech and First Amendment Theory*, 74 Nw.U.L. Rev. 372 (1979). *Also see FCC v. Pacifica Foundation*, 438 U.S. 726, 745-746 (1978) (opinion of Stevens, J.,): "The question in this case is whether a broadcast of patently offensive words dealing with sex and excretion may be regulated because of its content. Obscene materials have been denied the protection of the First Amendment because their content is so offensive to contemporary moral standards. *Roth v. United States*, 354 U.S. 476. But the fact that society may find speech offensive is not a sufficient reason for suppressing it. Indeed, if it is the speaker's opinion that gives offense, that consequence is a reason for according it constitutional protection. For it is a central tenet of the First Amendment that the government must remain neutral in the marketplace of ideas. If there were any reason to believe that the Commission's characterization of the Carlin monologue as offensive could be traced to its political content—or even to the fact that it satirized contemporary attitudes about four-letter words—First Amendment protection might be required. But that is simply not the case. These words offend for the same reason that obscenity offends. Their place in the hierarchy of First Amendment values was aptly sketched by Mr. Justice Murphy when he said: '[S]uch utterances are no essential part of any exposition of ideas, and are of such slight social value as a step of truth that any benefit that may be derived from them is clearly outweighed by the social interest in order and morality.' *Chaplinsky v. New Hampsire*, 315 U.S. at 572 (1942)."

29. *Noto v. United States*, 367 U.S. 290, 297-298 (1961). *See also Brandenburg v. Ohio*, 395 U.S. 444 (1969); *NAACP v. Claiborne Hardware*, 458 U.S. 886, 928 (1982).

30. *Brandenburg v. Ohio*, 395 U.S. 444, 447 (1969).

31. *New York Times v. Sullivan*, 376 U.S. 254, 270 (1964).

32. *Cantwell v. Connecticut*, 310 U.S. 296, 308 (1940).

33. *Feiner v. New York*, 340 U.S. 315, 321 (1951).

34. 357 U.S. 449 (1958).

35. *Id.* at 460 as cited in *NAACP v. Claiborne Hardware*, 458 U.S. 886, 908 (1982).

36. *DeJonge v. Oregon*, 299 U.S. 353, 365 (1937).

37. *Citizens Against Rent Control v. Berkeley*, 454 U.S. 290, 294 (1981).

38. *Id.*

39. 299 U.S. 353 (1937).

40. *Id.* at 365, as cited in *NAACP v Claiborne Hardware*, 458 U.S. 886, 908-909 (1982).
41. *NAACP v Claiborne Hardware*, 458 U.S. 886, 908 (1982).
42. 458 U.S. 886 (1982).
43. *Id.* at 920. *Cf. Scales v United States*, 367 U.S. 203, 229 (1961) ("blanket prohibition of association with a group having both legal and illegal aims would present a real danger that legitimate political expression or association would be impaired"); *Healy v James*, 408 U.S. 169, 185-86 (1972) ("the Court has consistently disapproved governmental action imposing . . . sanctions . . . solely because of a citizen's association with an unpopular organization"). *Also see Noto v United States*, 367 U.S. 290, 299 (1961); *United States v Robel*, 389 U.S. 258, 265 (1967).
44. 381 U.S. 301 (1965).
45. *Id.* at 308 (Brennan, J., concurring).
46. Comment, *The Right to Receive and Commercial Speech Doctrine: New Constitutional Considerations*, 63 Geo. L.J. 775, 777-778 (1975).
47. *Id. See, e.g., Martin v City of Struthers*, 319 U.S. 141, 143 (1943); *New York Times Co. v Sullivan*, 376 U.S. 254, 272 (1964); *Lamont v Postmaster General*, 381 U.S. 301, 305 (1965); *Griswold v Connecticut*, 381 U.S. 479, 482 (1965); *Stanley v Georgia*, 394 U.S. 557, 564 (1969); *Linmark Associates, Inc., v Willingboro, Township*, 431 U.S. 85 (1977).
48. *First National Bank of Boston v Bellotti*, 435 U.S. 765, 783 (1978); *Board of Education, Island Trees, Etc. v Pico*, 457 U.S. 853, 866 (1982) (plurality opinion).
49. *Stanley v Georgia*, 394 U.S. 557, 564 (1969); *Board of Education, Island Trees, Etc. v Pico*, 457 U.S. 853, 867 (1982). *See also Kleindienst v Mandel*, 408 U.S. 753, 762-763 (1972).
50. 457 U.S. 853 (1982).
51. *Id.* at 867.
52. *Id.*, citing *Martin v City of Struthers*, 319 U.S. 141, 143 (1943). *See also Lamont v Postmaster General*, 381 U.S. 301, 308 (1965), (Brennan, J., concurring).
53. *Id. Cf.* Alexander Meiklejohn, *Free Speech and Its Relation to Self-Government* 26 (1948); *Butler v Michigan*, 352 U.S. 380, 383-384 (1957); *Procunier v Martinez*, 416 U.S. 396, 408-409 (1974); *Houchins v KQED*, 438 U.S. 1, 30 (1978) (Stevens, J., dissenting); *Saxbe v Washington Post Co.*, 417 U.S. 843, 862-863 (1974) (Powell, J., dissenting).
54. *Red Lion Broadcasting Co. v FCC*, 395 U.S. 367, 386-390 (1969) (emphasis supplied). *See also Kleindienst v Mandel*, 408 U.S. 753, 763 (1972).

Chapter 3: The Historical Origins of the Freedom of Expression
1. Leon Whipple, *Our Ancient Liberties* 86 (New York: Da Capo Press, 1970).

2. In 1671, Sir William Berkeley of Virginia noted: "Thank God, we have neither free school nor printing-press, and I hope may not for a hundred years to come." *Id.* at 87.
3. Joseph Story, III *Commentaries on the Constitution of the United States* 734 (Boston, Mass.: Hillard, Gray, and Co., 1833).
4. *See generally* Zechariah Chafee, *Free Speech in the United States* 18-21 (Cambridge, Mass.: Harvard University Press, 1941).
5. John Lofton, *The Press as Guardian of the First Amendment.* 4 (Columbia, S.C.: South Carolina Press, 1980).
6. Chafee, *supra* note 4, at 20-21. *Cf.* Leonard W. Levy, *Legacy of Suppression: Freedom of Speech and Press in Early American History* 236-237 (Cambridge, Mass.: Belknap Press of Harvard University, 1960).
7. 3 *Annals of Cong.* 934 (1794).
8. "Address to the inhabitants of Quebec, 1774" from 1 *Journals of the Continental Congress, 1774-1789,* 108, as reproduced in Bernard Schwartz, 1 *The Bill of Rights: A Documentary History* 221-227 (New York: Chelsea House Publishers, 1971).
9. Arthur M. Schlesinger, "Liberty Trees: A Genealogy," 25 *The New England Quarterly* 435-438 (Portland, Maine: Anthoensen Press, 1952). Schlesinger notes many possible origins for the Liberty Tree: "As early as 1652 the Massachusetts authorities minted a shilling with the bas-relief (presumably) of a pine tree, and about fifty years later a pine-tree flag came into use. Meanwhile, outstanding historical incidents hallowed particular trees. At Annapolis, Maryland, a tulip poplar became famous as marking the spot where the Indians in 1652 had agreed to open the Chesapeake region to settlement; in Connecticut a tree in Hartford won renown as the Charter Oak because the colonial charter had supposedly been hidden there in 1687 to prevent its seizure by Sir Edmund Andros for King James II; and in Pennsylvania the people honored the Treaty Elm under which William Penn in 1683 had concluded a long-term peace with the Indians. The old English practice of the Maypole—a sort of denuded tree—may also have had an influence upon the colonists for, as we shall see, in the critical decade before 1776 they often used a Liberty Pole as a substitute for the Liberty Tree." *Id.* at 436-37.
10. 2 *Works of John Adams* 194 (Freeport, N.Y.: Books for Libraries Press, 1969).
11. The Dedham "Liberty Tree" was an eight-foot wooden pillar set upon a four-foot granite block. Crowning the pillar was a bust of William Pitt honoring him because he had "saved America from impending slavery" by pushing for the repeal of the Stamp Act. Charles Warren, *Jacobin and Junto* 33-34 (New York: AMS Press, 1970).
12. Newport's Liberty Tree was to be "emblematical of Public Liberty . . . in all Times and Ages forever hereafter." Roderick Terry,

"The History of the Liberty Tree of Newport," 27 *Newport Historical Society Bulletin* 9-12 (1918).

13. Schlesinger recounts that this Liberty Pole was replaced on five separate occasions. Schlesinger, *supra* note 9 at 441-46. The last of these, "[w]hen erected, . . . stood fourty-six (sic) feet supporting a gilt vane bearing the word 'Liberty.' For safety's sake the Sons braced this new 'Monument of Freedom' with iron hoops and vertical iron strips and sank it twelve feet below the surface." *Id.* at 446.

14. *Id.* at 445.

15. *Id.*

16. *Id.*

17. *Id.* at 449: "Three miscreants in Sandwich, who destroyed the Liberty Pole one night, were forced publicly to confess that they had behaved 'most Wickedly, Maliciously and Injuriously, (being instigated by the Devil, and our own evil hearts)' as well as to pay damages." *Id.*

18. *Id.* at 450.

19. Liberty caps, of Gallic origins, were probably representative of the Phrygian headpiece which was given to a slave upon his emancipation.

20. *Id.* at 445.

21. *Id.* at 456.

22. *Id.* at 457.

23. Robert Allen Rutland, *The Birth of the Bill of Rights* 89 (New York: Collier Books, 1962).

24. 1 Anson Phelps Stokes, *Church and State in the United States* 340 (New York: Harper & Bros., 1950).

25. 1 William T. Hutchinson and William E. Rachal, eds., *The Papers of James Madison* 106 (Chicago, Ill.: University of Chicago Press, 1962).

26. David Freeman Hawke, *Paine* 44 (New York: Harper & Row, 1974).

27. 2 William M. Van der Weyde, ed., *The Life and Works of Thomas Paine* 184-185 (New Rochelle, N.Y.: Thomas Paine National Historical Association, 1925).

28. *Id.*, Vol. 1 at 30-31.

29. Thomas Paine's *The Crisis* papers were first published on December 19, 1776 and were reissued one week later as a pamphlet. 2 *The Annals of America* 456-457 (Chicago, Ill.: Encyclopedia Britannica, Inc., 1968).

30. *See* 1 Stat. 596 (1978); 1 Stat. 570 (1978).

31. Leon Whipple, *Our Ancient Liberties* 28 (New York: Da Capo Press, 1970).

32. *Id.* at 51.

33. *Id.*

34. Russel Blaine Nye, *Fettered Freedom: Civil Liberties and the Slavery Controversy, 1830 through 1860* 174-177 (East Lansing, Mich: Michigan State University Press, 1964).

35. *See generally* Leon Whipple, *The Story of Civil Liberties in the United States* 84-124 (New York: Vanguard Press, 1927), for a detailed account of such intolerance.
36. John Lofton, *The Press as Guardian of the First Amendment* 80 (Columbia, S.C.: University of South Carolina Press, 1980).
37. *Id.* at 80-81.
38. Whipple, *supra* note 32 at 89,
39. *Id.* at 81.
40. Harold L. Nelson, ed., *Freedom of the Press from Hamilton to the Warren Court* 216-217 (New York: Bobbs-Merrill Co., 1967).
41. Whipple, *supra* note 32 at 106.
42. *Id.* at 104.
43. In the eleven weeks following the firing upon Fort Sumter of April 12, 1861, thousands of American citizens were arrested and held without trial by the Union Army. President Abraham Lincoln, under the color of executive power, suspended the writ of habeas corpus until such a time as a special session of Congress could be called upon July 4, 1861. This suspension "caused persons who were represented to him as being or about to engage in disloyal and treasonable practices to be arrested by special civil as well as military agencies and detained in military agencies to prevent them or deter others from such practices." James D. Richardson, III *A Compilation of the Messages and Papers of the Presidents* 3304 (New York: Bureau of National Literature, 1897). The reason that Lincoln chose to suspend the writ of habeas corpus rather than wait for another "Sedition Act" was clear:

> Legislation applying to all alike would have been unjust and alienating to the border state doubters, and would have been widely criticized as an illustration of the despotism so often charged against Lincoln by his opponents. But, without the sanction of the legislation, the federal government arrested by the thousands men whom it knew or suspected to be dangerous or disaffected, and confined them without charges and without trial in military prisons as long as it saw fit—and public opinion generally acquiesced in this as a fairly necessary measure of wartime precaution. The number of such executive arrests has been variously estimated up to as high as 38,000. The War Department records, confessedly very incomplete, show over 13,000.

Hall, *Free Speech in Wartime*, 21 Colum. L. Rev. 527 (1921). Later, in the Act of March 3, 1863 (12 Stat. 755 [1863]), Congress ratified Lincoln's suspension of the requirement of a writ of habeas corpus. The federal judiciary, however, gave Lincoln's actions a mixed review. Chief Justice Roger Taney, while riding the Circuit in Baltimore, held that Lincoln could not suspend the writ of habeas corpus. *See Ex Parte Merryman*, 17 F. Cas. 144 (C.C. Md. 1861) (No. 9,487). Attorney General Bates upheld

Lincoln's right to do so. Suspension of the privilege of the writ of habeas corpus, 10 Op. Att'y. Gen. 74 (1861).

44. Howard Wayne Morgan, *Eugene V. Debs, Socialist for President* 138 (Syracuse, N.Y.: Syracuse University Press, 1962).

45. Espionage Act of 1917, tit. I, SS 3, 4, and 5, 40 Stat. 219 (1917), Amendment of May 16, 1918 to S 3 of the Espionage Act of June 15, 1917, 40 Stat. 553 (1918).

46. 40 Stat. 553 (1918). Repealed 41 Stat. 1359-1360 (1921).

47. *Id.* Under a parallel Minnesota Espionage Act it had been held a crime to discourage women from knitting by remarking, "No soldier ever sees these socks." *State v. Freerks,* 140 Minn. 349, 168 N.W. 23 (1918).

48. Ray Ginger, *The Bending Cross: A Biography of Eugene Victor Debs* 350 (New Brunswick, N.J.: Rutgers University Press, 1949).

49. *Debs v. United States,* 249 U.S. 211, 214 (1919).

50. 249 U.S. 211 (1919). *Also see Schenck v. United States,* 249 U.S. 47 (1919); *Abrams v. United States* 250 U.S. 616 (1919).

51. Morgan, *supra* note 44 at 164.

52. *Id.* at 189.

53. *Id.* at 177.

54. Clinton Rossiter, Joseph M. Snee, and Arthur E. Sutherland eds., *Digest of the Public Record of Communism in the United States* 188 (New York: The Fund for the Republic, 1955).

55. 249 U.S. 47 (1919).

56. 250 U.S. 616 (1919).

57. *Id.* at 621.

58. Rossiter, Snee, and Sutherland, *supra* note 54 at 191.

59. 251 U.S. 466 (1920).

60. 252 U.S. 239 (1920).

61. *Id.* at 247.

62. 255 U.S. 22 (1921).

63. Rossiter, Snee, and Sutherland, *supra* note 54 at 192.

64. The Smith Act is the informal name for the Alien Registration Act of 1940, 54 Stat. 670 (1940), 18 U.S.C. S 2385 (Supp. 1952).

65. One of the earliest convictions under the Smith Act was *Dunne v. United States,* 138 F. 2d 137 (8th Cir. 1943), *cert. denied* 320 U.S. 790 (1943), in which eighteen members of the Socialist Workers Party from Minnesota were convicted for conspiracy under the Smith Act. Evidence showed that Teamster's Local No. 544 had formed a military organization known as the "Defense Guards" to overthrow the government. Marxist literature was disseminated by them and they maintained contact with Leon Trotsky, then in Mexico. Thus, their conviction was upheld.

The first case to be heard by the United States Supreme Court under the Smith Act was *Dennis v. United States,* 341 U.S. 494 (1951). In this case, the Court finding that the petitioners intended to overthrow the United States Government "as speedily as circumstances would permit" distorted somewhat Holmes's "clear and present danger" test to uphold the convictions. *Id.* at

509-11. The Court construed this test to determine "whether the gravity of the 'evil,' discounted by its improbability, justifies such invasion of free speech as is necessary to avoid the danger." *Id.* at 510.

Yates u United States, 354 U.S. 298 (1957), involved fourteen lower echelon Communist leaders' convictions under the Smith Act's "organization clause." The trial court gave the term "organize" a broad meaning, including the advocacy of abstract doctrine as well as actions within the prohibitions. In *Yates* it is clearly established that advocacy and teaching of forcible overthrow of government as an abstract principle is immune from prosecution. *Id.* at 318.

Later, *Scales u United States*, 367 U.S. 203 (1961), and *Noto u United States*, 367 U.S. 290 (1961), clarified that mere membership in subversive organizations is not punishable. Only an active member who has knowledge of a plan to overthrow the government by violence and intends to participate therein may be prosecuted.

Chapter 4: Self-Expression in Public: The Development of a Right

1. 268 U.S. 652 (1925).
2. *Id.* at 669.
3. *Id.* at 673 (Holmes, J., and Brandeis, J., dissenting).
4. "Criminal syndicalism" was defined by the Oregon statute as "the doctrine which advocates crime, physical violence, sabotage or any unlawful acts or methods as a means of accomplishing or effecting industrial or political change or revolution." Oregon Code, 1930, SS14-3110-3112, as amended by chapter 459, Oregon Laws, 1933.
5. 299 U.S. 353 (1937).
6. *Id.* at 364-365.
7. *Id.*
8. 303 U.S. 444 (1938).
9. *Id.* at 451.
10. *Id.* at 452.
11. 307 U.S. 496 (1939).
12. *Id.* at 515-516.
13. 308 U.S. 147 (1940).
14. *Id.* at 160-161.
15. *Id.* at 162.
16. 312 U.S. 569 (1941).
17. 308 U.S. 147, 160-161 (1940).
18. 312 U.S. at 574 (1941).
19. 315 U.S. 568 (1942).
20. *Id.* at 572.
21. *Id.* at 574.
22. 316 U.S. 52 (1942).
23. 318 U.S. 413 (1943).
24. *Id.* at 417.

25. 318 U.S. 422 (1943).
26. *Id.* at 423-424.
27. 319 U.S. 105 (1943).
28. *Id.* at 109.
29. *Id.* at 111.
30. *Id.* at 115.
31. 319 U.S. 141 (1943).
32. *Id.* at 144.
33. *Id.* at 146-147.
34. 321 U.S. 158 (1944).
35. *Id.* at 169-170.
36. 321 U.S. 573 (1944).
37. *Id.* at 576-577.
38. 323 U.S. 516 (1945).
39. *Id.* at 529-530 (emphasis supplied).
40. 340 U.S. 268 (1951).
41. *Id.* at 272.
42. *Id.* at 273.
43. 340 U.S 290 (1951).
44. *Id.* at 292.
45. Justice Robert Jackson in his dissent notes: "At the meetings, Kunz preached, among many other things of like tenor, that 'The Catholic Church makes merchandise out of souls,' that Catholicism is 'a religion of the devil,' and that the Pope is 'the anti-Christ.' The Jews he denounced as 'Christ-Killers,' and he said of them, 'All the garbage that didn't believe in Christ should have been burnt in the incinerators. It's a shame they all weren't.' " *Id.* at 296 (Jackson, J., dissenting).
46. 307 U.S. 496 (1939).
47. *Id.* at 295.
48. A "Green River ordinance" is an anticanvassing regulation which forbids going in and upon private residences for the purpose of soliciting sales. This type of ordinance originated in Green River, Wyoming, in 1931.
49. 341 U.S. 622 (1951).
50. *Id.* at 645.
51. 345 U.S. 67 (1953).
52. *Id.* at 69.
53. 345 U.S. 395 (1953).
54. *Id.* at 414.
55. 425 U.S. 610 (1976).
56. 444 U.S. 620 (1980).
57. 425 U.S. 610 (1976).
58. 425 U.S. at 613, citing *Connally v. General Construction Co.,* 269 U.S. 385, 391 (1926).
59. 444 U.S. 620 (1980).
60. *Id.* at 633.
61. *Id.* at 636-637.
62. *Id.* at 638-639.

Chapter 5: The Outer Limits of Expression

1. Alexander Meiklejohn, *Political Freedom* 57 (New York: Harper and Row, 1960).
2. 394 U.S. 576 (1969).
3. *Id.* at 579.
4. *Id.* at. 578.
5. *Id.* at 593.
6. 395 U.S. 444 (1969).
7. *Id.* at 446.
8. 341 U.S. 494 (1951).
9. 367 U.S. 290 (1961).
10. 341 U.S. at 507.
11. 367 U.S. at 297-298.
12. 415 U.S. 566 (1974).
13. *Id.* at 568.
14. 418 U.S. 405 (1974).
15. 69 Ill. 2d 605, 373 N.E. 2d 21 (1978).
16. 373 N.E. 2d at 22. *Also see Village of Skokie v National Socialist Party of America*, 51 Ill. App. 3d 279, 366 N.E. 2d 347, 350 (1977).
17. Village Ordinance No. 77-5-N-994.
18. Village Ordinance No. 77-5-N-995, S28-43.2.
19. Village Ordinance No. 77-5-N-996.
20. *See Collin v Smith*, 447 F. Supp. 676 (E.D. Ill. 1978); *Collin v Smith*, 578 F. 2d 1197 (7th Cir. 1978), *cert. denied* 439 U.S. 916 (1978).
21. *National Socialist Party of America v Village of Skokie*, 432 U.S. 43 (1977).
22. *Id.* at 44.
23. *Village of Skokie v National Socialist Party of America*, 51 Ill. App. 3d 279, 293, 366 N.E. 2d 347, 357 (1977).
24. *Village of Skokie v National Socialist Party of America*, 69 Ill. 2d 605, 373 N.E. 2d 21 (1978)
25. 69 Ill. 2d at 615, 373 N.E. 2d at 24.
26. 373 N.E. 2d at 26.
27. For an overview of the entire case and its ramifications in a democratic nation, *see* Irving Louis Horowitz and Victoria Curtis Bramson, *Skokie, the ACLU and the Endurance of Democratic Theory,* 43 Law and Contemp. Problems 328 (Duke) (1979).
28. Lyles, *Skokie as a Symbol*, 95 Christian Century 412 (1978).

Chapter 6: Picketing: The Historical Perspective

1. *Keith Theatre v Vachon*, 134 Me. 392, 187 A. 692 (1936). *See also Elkind & Sons v Retail Clerks*, 114 N.J. Eq. 586, 169 A. 494 (1933); Feinberg, *Picketing, Free Speech and "Labor Disputes,"* 17 N.Y.U.L. Rev. 385, 394 (1940).
2. *Atchinson T. & S. F. Ry. Co. v Gee*, 139 F. 582 (C.C. S.D. Iowa E.D. 1905).
3. 45 Mass. (4 Met.) 111 (Mass.1842).

4. *Id.* at 134 (emphasis supplied).
5. 257 U.S. 184 (1921).
6. *Id.* at 207.
7. *Id.* at 205.
8. *Id.*
9. 8 Harv. L. Rev. 1 (1894).
10. 167 Mass. 92, 44 N.E. 1077 (1896).
11. 176 Mass. 492, 57 N.E. 1011 (1900).
12. Felix Frankfurter and Nathan Greene, *The Labor Injunction* 24 (Gloucester, Mass.: P. Smith Publishers, 1930).
13. *Vegelahn v. Gunter,* 167 Mass. 92, 105, 44 N.E. 1077, 1080 (Mass. 1896).
14. *Senn v. Tile Layers Protective Union,* 301 U.S. 468 (1937).
15. *New Negro Alliance v. Sanitary Grocery Co.,* 303 U.S. 552 (1938).
16. 4 Sand. Ch. 357 (N.Y. 1846).
17. *Truax v. Corrigan,* 257 U.S. 312 (1921).
18. 147 Mass. 212, 17 N.E. 307 (1888).
19. 310 U.S. 88 (1940).
20. *Id.* at 104.
21. *Id.* at 104-105. *Cf. Schenck v. United States,* 249 U.S. 47, 52 (1919) (Holmes, J., dissenting).
22. 257 U.S. 184 (1921).
23. 310 U.S. 88, 105 (1940).
24. The earliest United States Supreme Court discussion of the idea of "preferred freedoms" occurred in the case of *Calder v. Bull,* 3 U.S. (3 Dall.) 386 (1798). Justice Samuel Chase, relying heavily upon sixteenth- and seventeenth-century concepts of a higher or natural law, believed that the framers of the Constitution intended government to be limited by natural law as well as by written constitutional restrictions. Chase, therefore, believed it was the duty of the Supreme Court to invalidate legislation which interfered with the traditional natural law rights of the individual. *Id.* at 386-387. Although Chase's views were largely rejected by the early Supreme Court, in later years analogous reasoning prevailed. For example, Chief Justice Harlan Stone, in *United States v. Carolene Products Company,* 304 U.S. 144 (1938), inscribed the now famous footnote 4 of that opinion. He wrote: "There may be a narrower scope for operation of the presumption of constitutionality when legislation appears on its face to be within a specific prohibition of the Constitution, such as those of the first ten amendments, which are deemed equally specific when held to be embraced within the Fourteenth." *Id.* at 152 n. 4.
25. 319 U.S. 105 (1943).
26. *Id.* at 115. *See also Herndon v. Lowry,* 301 U.S. 242, 258 (1937); *Thornhill v. Alabama,* 310 U.S. 88, 95 (1940); *Schneider v. State,* 308 U.S. 147, 161 (1939); *Bridges v. California,* 314 U.S. 252, 262-263 (1941); *Prince v. Massachusetts,* 321 U.S. 158, 164 (1943); *Follett v. McCormick,* 321 U.S. 573, 575 (1943); *Marsh v. Alabama,* 326 U.S. 501, 509 (1945); *Saia v. New York,* 334 U.S. 558, 562 (1947); *West Virginia State Board of Education v. Barnette,*

319 U.S. 624, 639 (1943); *Thomas v. Collins,* 323 U.S. 516, 530 (1945).

27. *Edwards v. South Carolina,* 372 U.S. 229, 235 (1963).
28. *Cox v. Louisiana,* 379 U.S. 559, 566 (1965).

Chapter 7: Picketing as Free Expression: The Modern Development

1. 379 U.S. 536 (1965).
2. *Id.* at 555.
3. 315 U.S. 769 (1942).
4. *Id.* at 776-777 (Douglas, J., concurring). *Cf. Giboney v. Empire Storage and Ice Co.,* 336 U.S. 490, 502 (1949), where Justice Black wrote: "It has never been deemed an abridgment of freedom of speech or press to make a course of conduct illegal merely because the conduct was in part initiated, evidenced, or carried out by means of language, either spoken, written, or printed." Justice Douglas later concurred, "Picketing is free speech-*plus*, the *plus* being physical activity that may implicate traffic and related matters. Hence the later aspects of picketing may be regulated." *Amalgamated Food Employees Union, Local 590 v. Logan Valley Plaza,* 391 U.S. 308, 326 (1968). Justice Frankfurter, writing in *Hughes v. Superior Court,* 339 U.S. 460, 465 (1950), closely followed Justice Douglas's reasoning in stating that "the very purpose of a picket line is to exert influences, and it produces consequences, different from other modes of communication. The loyalties and responses evoked and exacted by picket lines are unlike those flowing from appeals by printed word."
5. 391 U.S. 367 (1968).
6. *Id.* at 376. The Court continues: "To characterize the quality of the governmental interest which must appear, the Court has employed a variety of descriptive terms: compelling; substantial; subordinating; paramount; cogent; strong. Whatever imprecision inheres in these terms, we think it clear that a government regulation is sufficiently justified if it is within the constitutional power of Government; if it furthers an important or substantial governmental interest; if the governmental interest is *unrelated to the suppression of free expression;* and if the incidental restriction on alleged First Amendment freedoms is no greater than is essential to the furtherance of that interest." *Id.* (emphasis supplied). *Cf. NAACP v. Claiborne Hardware,* 458 U.S. 886, 912, n. 47 (1982).
7. 310 U.S. 88 (1940).
8. *Id.* at 94. The employee testified that he was neither intimidated nor frightened by Thornhill's statement. He testified to the picketers' and Thornhill's peaceful demeanor. *Id.* at 94-95.
9. *Id.* at 104.
10. *Id.* at 105. *But cf.* Etelson, *Picketing and Freedom of Speech: Comes the Evolution,* 10 J. Mar. J. Prac. & Proc. 1, 3 (1976): "The alleged misconduct in the case merely involved a direct, non-

threatening request by Byron Thornhill to a fellow employee asking him to support the union strike by not entering the premises. The actual holding, therefore, went no further than to establish constitutional protection for that aspect of the picketing which was indisputably 'speech.' "

11. *See, e.g., Teamsters, Local 695 v Vogt, Inc.,* 354 U.S. 284 (1957); *Garner v Teamsters, Local 776,* 346 U.S. 485 (1953); *Journeymen Plumbers v Graham,* 345 U.S. 192 (1953); *Building Servs. Employees Int'l Union v Gazzam,* 339 U.S. 532 (1950); *Teamsters v Hanke,* 339 U.S. 470 (1950); *Hughes v Superior Court,* 339 U.S. 460 (1950); *Giboney v Empire Storage & Ice Co.,* 336 U.S. 490 (1949); *Cafeteria Employees Union, Local 302 v Angelos,* 320 U.S. 293 (1943); *Bakery & Pastry Drivers Local 802 v Wohl,* 315 U.S. 769 (1942); *Carpenters & Joiners Union of America, Local 213 v Ritter's Cafe,* 315 U.S. 722 (1942); *AFL v Swing,* 312 U.S. 321 (1941). *Also see* Etelson, *Picketing and Freedom of Speech: Comes the Evolution,* 10 J. Mar. J. Prac. & Proc. 1, 3 (1976); Jones, *The Right to Picket—Twilight Zone of the Constitution,* 102 U. Pa. L. Rev. 995 (1954).

12. 336 U.S. 490 (1949).

13. *Id.* at 502 (emphasis supplied).

14. *Id.* at 498. "[P]lacards used as an essential and inseparable part of a grave offense . . . cannot immunize that unlawful conduct from state control." *Id.* at 502.

15. *NAACP v Claiborne Hardware,* 458 U.S. 886, 912 (1982). *Cf. NLRB v Retail Store Employees Union,* 447 U.S. 607, 614 (1980) (a secondary consumer boycott is forbidden if it "threatens neutral parties with ruin or substantial loss").

16. 354 U.S. 284 (1957).

17. *Id.* at 291.

18. *Id.* at 289. Frankfurter viewed *Vogt* as a "review of the balance struck by a State between picketing that involved more than 'publicity' and competing interests of state policy." *Id.* at 290.

19. *Id.* at 293.

20. Justices Douglas and Black were the authors of the "speech-*plus* analysis and *Giboney* respectively. Etelson, *Picketing and Freedom of Speech: Comes the Evolution,* 10 J. Mar. J. Prac. & Proc. 1, 7 (1976).

21. 419 U.S. 215 (1974).

22. *Id.* at 229; *Teamsters, Local 695 v Vogt, Inc.,* 354 U.S. 284, 290 (1957).

23. 377 U.S. 58 (1964).

24. A secondary boycott is any picketing activity aimed at a business not directly involved in a labor dispute with the boycotting union. Federal statute forbids this type of conduct, 29 U.S.C. & 158(b)(4)(ii)(B)(1976). Thus, a primary boycott is one in which economic pressure is brought to bear directly upon the business or group with whom the boycotters have their principal dispute. A secondary boycott involves the use of economic pressure

against a neutral party in an attempt to force that party to align
against the primary target.
25. 377 U.S. 58, 63 (1964).
26. 408 U.S. 92 (1972).
27. "We accept Mr. Justice Black's quoted views. *Cf. NLRB v. Fruit &
Vegetable Packers [Tree Fruits]*, 377 U.S. 58, 76 (1964) (Black, J.,
concurring)." *Id.* at 98.
28. 377 U.S. 58, 77-78 (1964).
29. 372 U.S. 229 (1963).

Chapter 8: Antidiscrimination Picketing: Strengthening the Right
1. *Edwards v. South Carolina*, 372 U.S. 229, 235 (1963).
2. *Id.* at 230-231.
3. *Id.* at 236. Justice Stewart distinguished this situation from that
in *Feiner v. New York*, 340 U.S. 315 (1951), where the situation
was clearly more volatile.
4. *Id.* at 237.
5. 372 U.S. 229 (1963).
6. *Id.* at 235.
7. *Cox v. Louisiana*, 379 U.S. 536 (1965) *(Cox I);* and, *Cox v. Louisiana*, 379 U.S. 559 (1965) *(Cox II)*.
8. 379 U.S. 536 (1965) *(Cox I)*.
9. 379 U.S. 559 (1965) *(Cox II)*.
10. *Cox v. Louisiana*, 379 U.S. 536, 552 (1965) *(Cox I)*, *citing Terminiello v. Chicago*, 337 U.S. 1, 4-5 (1949).
11. *Id.* at 552.
12. *Id.* at 558.
13. La. Rev. Stat., 14:401 (Cum. Supp. 1962).
14. *Cox v. Louisiana*, 379 U.S. 559, 566 (1965) *(Cox II)*. The Court
noted: "The conduct which is the subject of this statute—picketing and parading—is subject to regulation even though intertwined with expression and association." *Id.* at 563, *citing Hughes
v. Superior Court*, 339 U.S. 460 (1950); *Giboney v. Empire Storage
& Ice Co.*, 336 U.S. 490 (1949); *Building Service Employees v.
Gazzam*, 339 U.S. 532 (1950). The Court then instructs, "But *cf.
Thornhill v. Alabama*, 310 U.S. 88 (1940)." *Cox v. Louisiana*, 379
U.S. 559, 563 (1965) *(Cox II)*.
15. *Id.* at 566.
16. *Id.* at 564, *citing Giboney v. Empire Storage & Ice Co.*, 336 U.S. 490,
501-502 (1949).
17. *Id.* at 574, citing *NAACP v. Button*, 371 U.S. 415, 433 (1963).
18. *Id.* at 575-584.
19. *Id.* at 577.
20. *Cox v. Louisiana*, 379 U.S. 559, 564 (1965) *(Cox II)*, citing *Giboney
v. Empire Storage & Ice Co.*, 336 U.S. 490, 502 (1949), for the
proposition that "we are reviewing a statute narrowly drawn to
punish specific conduct that infringes a substantial state interest
in protecting the judicial process."
21. 383 U.S. 131 (1966).

22. *Id.* at 141-142.
23. 390 U.S. 611 (1968).
24. Miss. Code. Ann., 2318.5 (Supp. 1966).
25. 390 U.S. 611, 617 (1968), citing *Cox v Louisiana,* 379 U.S. 559, 563 (1965) *(Cox II).*
26. *Id.* at 617, citing *Schneider v State,* 308 U.S. 147, 161 (1939).
27. 394 U.S. 111 (1969).
28. 394 U.S. 147, 152 (1969).
29. *Id.*
30. 408 U.S. 92 (1972).
31. *Id.* at 95.
32. *Id.* at 99.
33. 447 U.S. 455 (1980).
34. *Id.* at 460-461.
35. *Id.* at 460. *See also Hague v CIO,* 307 U.S. 496, 515 (1939); *Hudgens v NLRB,* 424 U.S. 507, 515 (1976).
36. *Id.* at 466-467.
37. Thomas Emerson, *The System of Freedom of Expression* 444-449 (New York: Random House, Publishers, 1970).
38. 458 U.S. 886, 913 (1983).
39. *United States v Grace,* 461 U.S. _____ , 103 S. Ct. 1702 (April 20, 1983).
40. 40 U.S.C., 13K.
41. 461 U.S. _____ , 103 S. Ct. 1702, 1704 (April 20, 1983).
42. 461 U.S. _____ , 103 S. Ct. 1702, 1707 (April 20, 1983).
43. *Id.* (emphasis supplied).

Chapter 9: Picketing and Public Property

1. *Pruneyard Shopping Center v Robins,* 447 U.S. 74, 82 (1980). *See also Kaiser Aetna v United States,* 444 U.S. 164, 179-80 (1979).
2. *United States v Grace,* 461 U.S. _____ , 103 S. Ct. 1702 (April 20, 1983); *Adderley v Florida,* 385 U.S. 39, 47-48 (1966).
3. *United States Postal Service v Greenburgh Civic Association,* 453 U.S. 114, 129 (1981).
4. *United States v Grace,* 461 U.S. _____ , 103 S. Ct. 1702, 1707 (April 20, 1983); *Greer v Spock,* 424 U.S. 828, 836 (1976).
5. 460 U.S. 37 (1983).
6. *Id.* at 45-47.
7. 461 U.S. _____ , 103 S. Ct. 1702 (April 20, 1983).
8. 40 U.S.C. 13K [40 U.S.C.S., 13K].
9. 461 U.S. _____ , 103 S. Ct. 1702, 1708 (April 20, 1983).
10. *Id. See also United States Postal Service v Greenburgh Civic Association,* 453 U.S. 114, 133 (1981).
11. 307 U.S. 496 (1939).
12. *Id.* at 515-516.
13. *Hudgens v NLRB,* 424 U.S. 507, 515 (1976). *Cf. Food Employees v Logan Valley Plaza,* 391 U.S. 308, 315 (1968); *Carey v Brown,* 447 U.S. 455, 460 (1980).
14. *United States v Grace,* 461 U.S. _____ , 103 S. Ct. 1702, 1708 (April 20, 1983).

15. 461 U.S. _____ , 103 S. Ct. 1702, 1707; *Perry Educational Association v. Perry Local Educators' Association*, 460 U.S. 37 (1983); *Widmar v. Vincent*, 454 U.S. 263 (1981).
16. *Thomas v. Collins*, 323 U.S. 516, 530 (1945).
17. *Perry Educational Association v. Perry Local Educators' Association*, 460 U.S. 37, 45 (1983).
18. 461 U.S. _____ , 103 S. Ct. 1702, 1707 (April 20, 1983).
19. 460 U.S. 37, 46 (1983); *Widmar v. Vincent*, 454 U.S. 263 (1981 (university meeting facilities); *City of Madison Joint School District v. Wisconsin Public Employment Relations Commission*, 429 U.S. 167 (1976) (school board meeting); *Southeastern Promotions, Ltd. v. Conrad*, 420 U.S. 546 (1975) (municipal theatre).
20. 460 U.S. 37, 46 n. 7 (emphasis supplied).
21. 454 U.S. 263 (1981).
22. 429 U.S. 167 (1976) *Cf. Perry Educational Association v. Perry Local Educators' Association*, 460 U.S. 37, 46 n. 7. *Also see Niemotko v. Maryland*, 340 U.S. 268 (1951); *Police Dept. of Chicago v. Mosley*, 408 U.S. 92 (1972); *City of Madison Joint School District v. Wisconsin Public Employment Relations Commission*, 429 U.S. 167 (1976); *Carey v. Brown*, 447 U.S. 455 (1980); *Widmar v. Vincent*, 454 U.S. 263 (1981); *Tinker v. Des Moines Independent Community School District*, 393 U.S. 503 (1969) (not the validity of an unequal access policy, but instead an unequivocal attempt to prevent students from expressing their viewpoint on a political issue).
23. 454 U.S. 263, 269-270 (1981). *Cf. Carey v. Brown*, 447 U.S. 455, 461, 464-465 (1980).
24. *Widmar v. Vincent*, 454 U.S. at 277.
25. *United States Postal Service v. Greenburgh Civic Association*, 453 U.S. 114, 129 (1981).
26. *Id.* at 129; *Adderley v. Florida*, 385 U.S. 39, 47 (1966); *Greer v. Spock*, 424 U.S. 828, 836 (1976).
27. 385 U.S. 39 (1966).
28. *Id.* at 45.
29. *Id.* at 45 n. 5.
30. *Id.* at 47. *Cf. Jones v. North Carolina Prisoners' Union*, 433 U.S. 119, 130-131 (1977).
31. 418 U.S. 298 (1974).
32. *Id.* at 302, 304.
33. *Consolidated Edison v. Public Service Commission*, 447 U.S. 530, 539 (1980).
34. 424 U.S. 828 (1976).
35. 453 U.S. 114 (1981).
36. *Also see Perry Educational Association v. Perry Local Educators' Association*, 460 U.S. 37 (1983), which applies the same rationale to teachers' unions use of a school's internal mail system. *Perry* most clearly defines the three categories of public forums which may exist on public property. *Id.* at 45-47.
37. *Id.* at 46, 47. Various reservations on these forums to their intended purpose are *Dallas Association of Community Organizations for Reform Now v. Dallas County Hospital District*, 670 F. 2d 629,

632 (5th Cir. 1982) ("the essence of time, place, or manner regulation lies in the recognition that various methods of speech, regardless of content, may frustrate legitimate government goals," thus, striking down a hospital's "no solicitation rule.") *Cf. NLRB v. Baptist Hospital, Inc.*, 442 U.S. 773, 787-788 (1979) ("solicitation in at least some of the public areas of hospitals often will not adversely affect patient care or disturb patients.") *See also* Redish, *The Content Distinction in First Amendment Analysis*, 34 Stan. L. Rev. 113 (1981).

Chapter 10: Picketing and Private Property

1. 326 U.S. 501 (1946).
2. *Id.* at 502-503. The Court also noted: "The town and the surrounding neighborhood, which cannot be distinguished from the Gulf property by anyone not familiar with the property lines, are thickly settled, and according to all indications the residents use the business block as their regular shopping center. To do so, they now, as they have for many years, make use of a company-owned paved street and sidewalk located alongside the store fronts in order to enter and leave the stores and the post office." *Id.* at 503.
3. *Id.* at 506 (emphasis supplied).
4. *Id.* at 508.
5. *Lloyd Corp. v. Tanner*, 407 U.S. 551, 569 (1972). *See also Hudgens v. NLRB*, 424 U.S. 507, 519 (1976).
6. 326 U.S. at 502.
7. 391 U.S. 308 (1968).
8. *Id.* at 318.
9. *Id.* at 319-320.
10. Justice Black explained: "But *Marsh* was never intended to apply to this kind of situation. *Marsh* dealt with the very special situation of a company-owned town, complete with streets, alleys, sewers, stores, residences, and everything else that goes to make a town. . . . I respectfully suggest that this reasoning completely misreads *Marsh* and begs the question. The question is, Under what circumstances can private property be treated as though it were public? The answer that *Marsh* gives is when that property has taken on *all* the attributes of a town." *Id.* at 330-332.
11. 407 U.S. 551 (1972).
12. *Id.* at 563 (emphasis supplied).
13. *Id.* at 565-566. A companion case to *Lloyd Corporation*, which was decided the same day by the Supreme Court and involved non-employee picketing of a hardware store, was *Central Hardware Company v. NLRB*, 407 U.S. 539 (1972). Central Hardware was a free-standing retail store surrounded by a parking lot owned by the company. In campaigning to organize the employees, the union made contact with employees in the parking lot. Management enforced its no-solicitation rule and caused a union organizer to be arrested. Charges were filed with the National Labor Relations Board by the union and the Board ultimately decided

in favor of the union. However, in deciding the case, reliance was placed upon *Amalgamated Foods v. Logan Valley Plaza,* 391 U.S. 308 (1968), rather than on *NLRB v. Babcok & Wilcox Co.,* 351 U.S. 105 (1956). The distinction was that *Logan Valley Plaza* was decided on constitutional grounds, whereas *Wilcox* was decided under Section 7 of the National Labor Relations Act, which provided for minimal infringement of property rights in order to participate in labor organization activities. The tenor of the opinion was that even under Section 7, property rights could be infringed in order to accommodate labor organization campaigning, *only when no alternative location would serve* to facilitate such activity. The Court in *Central Hardware* said: "Before an owner of private property can be subjected to the commands of the First and Fourteenth Amendments the privately owned property must assume to some significant degree the functional attributes of public property devoted to public use." 407 U.S. at 547.

14. 424 U.S. 507 (1976).
15. *Id.* at 518.
16. *Id.* at 523-524.
17. 447 U.S. 74 (1980).
18. *Id.* at 78.
19. *Id.* at 81.
20. *Id.* at 96.
21. *Id.* at 99-100. Whereas the United States Supreme Court upheld the California ruling in *Pruneyard* allowing free speech on private property, the North Carolina Supreme Court subsequently ruled the opposite. *See State v. Helmut,* 302 N.C. 173, 273 S.E. 2d 708 (1981).
22. Cases finding a quasi-public interest in otherwise excludable property include: *Wohlin v. Port of New York Authority,* 392 F. 2d 83 (2d Cir. 1968), *cert. denied* 393 U.S. 940 (1968) (bus terminal); *In re Hoffman,* 64 Cal. Rptr. 97, 434 P. 2d 353 (1967) (privately owned Los Angeles railroad station); *In re Lane,* 79 Cal. Rptr. 729, 457 P. 2d 561 (1969) (privately owned sidewalk in front of a supermarket open to the public); *Brown v. State of Louisiana,* 383 U.S. 131 (1966) (public library); *State v. Kolez,* 114 N.J. Super. 408, 276 A. 2d 595, 599 (1971) (privately owned retirement village "in many essential regards a self-sufficient community"); *Edwards v. South Carolina,* 372 U.S. 229 (1963) (site of the state government); *People v. De Clemente,* 442 N.Y.S. 2d 931 (N.Y. City Crim. Ct. 1981) (airport terminal); *State v. Schmid,* 84 N.J. 535, 423 A. 2d 615 (1980); *Commonwealth v. Tate,* 432 A. 2d 1382 (Pa. 1981) (auditorium of private college); *Teitelbaum v. Sorenson,* 648 F. 2d 1248 (9th Cir. 1981) (nursing home); *Cowley v. Tapley,* N.Y.S.C., Oneida County, December 22, 1983 (sidewalk in front of abortion clinic permitted); *State v. Barton,* No. 83-17739, 83-17341 (Phoenix Mun. Ct., September 20, 1982) (parking lot adjacent to abortion clinic). Clear guidelines in the abortion clinic context are appearing. *See O.B.G.Y.N. v. Birthright*

of Brooklyn and Queens, Inc., 64 A. 2d 894, 407 N.Y.S. 2d 903, 906 (1978) (picketing, counseling, and pamphleteering outside an abortion clinic are protected: "The message that defendants sought to communicate was an expression of their views about important public questions and policies entitled to the greatest constitutional protection"); *Gaetano v. United States,* 406 A. 2d 1291 (D.C. App. 1979) (blocking entrances to abortion chambers by a "sit-in" is not protected); *North Virginia Women's Medical Center v. Balch,* 617 F. 2d 1045 (1980) (blocking entrance to abortion clinic and to abortion chambers by a "sit-in" are not protected); *People v. Krizka,* 92 Ill. App. 3d 288, 416 N.E. 2d 36 (1980) (peaceful "interposition" of defendants between women seeking abortions and abortionists not protected); *People v. Stiso,* 416 N.E. 2d 1209 (Ill. App. 1981) (defendants forming a circle in waiting room to block access to abortion chambers not protected); *Cleveland v. Municipality of Anchorage,* 631 P. 2d 1073 (Alaska 1981) (defendants handcuffing and chaining themselves to abortion tables and "sitting-in" in waiting area not protected); *Grogan v. Beddiscombe,* 435 A. 2d 1069 (D.C. App. 1981) ("sit-in" in restricted area not protected); *City of St. Louis v. Klocker,* 637 S.W. 2d 174 (Mo. App. 1982) (blocking doorway to abortion procedure room not protected); *Parkmed v. Pro-Life Counselling, Inc.,* 110 Misc. 2d 369, 91 A. 2d 551 (1982) (picketing, pamphleting, carrying placards and prolife counseling permitted on steps in front of abortion clinic. The abortion clinic was on the twelfth floor of a thirty-four-story office building. Plaza immediately in front of the building is a proper forum); *Sigma Reproductive Health Center v. State,* 467 A. 2d 483 (Md. 1983) (reception area not a proper forum); *Feminist Women's Health Center v. Women Exploited by Abortion,* Memorandum decision No. 83-2-04142-8 (Snohomish County Super. Ct., May 13, 1984) (picketing protected as long as ingress and egress is not interfered with, i.e., visitors, patients, etc., should not have to "run . . . the gauntlet"). There are numerous other cases. As a general rule, *public sidewalk counseling* (as distinguished from on the sidewalks running directly into the abortion clinics) is protected, provided one remains in the public right of way.

Chapter 11: State Laws Concerning Picketing
1. 461 U.S. _____ , 103 S. Ct. 1702 (April 20, 1983).
2. 461 U.S. _____ , 103 S. Ct. 1702, 1707 (April 20, 1983) (emphasis supplied).
3. 447 U.S. 455 (1980) (emphasis supplied).
4. *Id.* at 460, *citing Hudgens v. NLRB,* 424 U.S. 507, 515 (1976); *Food Employees v. Logan Valley Plaza,* 391 U.S. 308, 315 (1968).
5. 408 U.S. 92 (1972).
6. *Id.* at 95-96. The Court continues: "[G]overnment may not grant the use of a forum to people whose views it finds acceptable, but deny use to those wishing to express less favored or more controversial views. . . . [I]t may not select which issues are worth

discussing. . . . There is an 'equality of status in the field of ideas.' " *Id.* at 96.

7. *Id.* at 98. *See also, Erznoznik v. City of Jacksonville,* 422 U.S. 205, 209 (1975); *Cox v. New Hampshire,* 312 U.S. 569 (1941); *Kovacs v. Cooper,* 336 U.S. 77 (1949); *Poulos v. New Hampshire,* 345 U.S. 395 (1953); *Grayned v. City of Rockford,* 408 U.S. 104 (1972).
8. 461 U.S. _____ , 103 S. Ct. 1702 (April 20, 1983).
9. 461 U.S. _____ , 103 S. Ct. 1702, 1707 (April 20, 1983).
10. 394 U.S. 147 (1969).
11. *Id.* at 153.
12. 340 U.S. 268 (1951).
13. *Id.* at 271.
14. *Shuttlesworth v. City of Birmingham,* 394 U.S. 147, 151 (1969).
15. 388 U.S. 307 (1967).
16. *Id.* at 321.
17. *Id.* at 315, 318.
18. *Cf. Poulos v. New Hampshire,* 345 U.S. 395 (1953); *Shuttlesworth v. Birmingham,* 394 U.S. 147, 151 (1969); *Wright v. Georgia,* 373 U.S. 284, 291-292 (1963).
19. *Organization for a Better Austin v. Keefe,* 402 U.S. 415, 419 (1971); *Carroll v. Princess Anne,* 393 U.S. 175, 181 (1968); *Bantam Books, Inc. v. Sullivan,* 372 U.S. 58, 70 (1963).
20. *Cox v. Louisiana,* 379 U.S. 536, 552 (1965). *See generally Cameron v. Johnson,* 390 U.S. 611 (1968); *Zwickler v. Koota,* 389 U.S. 241 (1967).
21. *Grayned v. City of Rockford,* 408 U.S. 104, 114-115 (1972).
22. 390 U.S. 611 (1968).
23. *Id.* at 616, *citing Connally v. General Construction Co.,* 269 U.S. 385, 391 (1926). *Also see* Schopler, *Annotation: Overbreadth—First Amendment* 45 L. Ed. 2d 725 (1975); *Zwickler v. Koota,* 389 U.S. 241 (1967); *United States v. Robel,* 389 U.S. 258 (1967); *Grayned v. Rockford,* 408 U.S. 104 (1972).
24. 379 U.S. 536 (1965).
25. *Id.* at 552.
26. 461 U.S. _____ , 103 S. Ct. 1702 (April 20, 1983).
27. 461 U.S. _____ , 103 S. Ct. 1702, 1707, *citing Perry Educational Association v. Perry Local Educators' Association,* 460 U.S. 37 (1983).
28. *Consolidated Edison Co. v. Public Service Commission,* 447 U.S. 530, 536 (1980).
29. *Grayned v. City of Rockford,* 408 U.S. 104, 116 (1972) (emphasis supplied). *Also see Brown v. Louisiana,* 383 U.S. 131 (1966); Wright, *The Constitution on the Campus,* 22 Vand. L. Rev. 1027, 1042 (1969). *Cf. Cox v. Louisiana,* 379 U.S. 559 (1965); *Adderley v. Florida,* 385 U.S. 39 (1966); *Food Employees v. Logan Valley Plaza,* 391 U.S. 308 (1968); *Tinker v. Des Moines Independent School District,* 393 U.S. 503 (1969); *Widmar v. Vincent,* 454 U.S. 263 (1981); *Heffron v. International Society for Krishna Consciousness, Inc.,* 452 U.S. 640 (1981). *Also see Dallas Association v. Dallas*

City Hospital, 670 F. 2d 629 (5th Cir. 1982) (hospital "no solicitation rule" invalid).

30. *Schneider v State,* 308 U.S. 147, 160-161 (1939).
31. *Cox v New Hampshire,* 312 U.S. 569, 576 (1941).
32. *Cf. Davis v Francois,* 395 F. 2d 730 (5th Cir. 1968) (picketing ordinance limiting number of picketers to two persons unconstitutional). *See generally Garcia v Gray,* 507 F. 2d 539 (10th Cir. 1974); *Baines v City of Danville,* 337 F. 2d 579 (4th Cir. 1964); *NAACP v Thompson,* 357 F. 2d 831 (5th Cir. 1966).
33. *Pritchard v Downie,* 326 F. 2d 323 (8th Cir. 1964) (cannot have riotous conduct); *United States v Aarons,* 310 F. 2d 341 (2d Cir. 1962) (cannot block launch of a vessel); *Hurwitt v City of Oakland,* 247 F. Supp. 995 (N.D. Calif. 1965) (cannot cordon off street and deny access to public or private building).
34. *Consolidated Edison Co. v Public Service Commission,* 447 U.S. 530, 536 (1980). *Also see Kovacs v Cooper,* 336 U.S. 77 (1949).
35. *Heffron v International Society for Krishna Consciousness, Inc.,* 452 U.S. 640, 648 (1981); *Consolidated Edison Co. v Public Service Commission,* 447 U.S. 530, 535 (1980); *Linmark Associates, Inc. v Willingboro Township,* 431 U.S. 85, 93 (1977); *Virginia Pharmacy Board v Virginia Citizens Consumer Council,* 425 U.S. 748, 771 (1976).
36. *Schneider v State,* 308 U.S. 147, 163 (1939); *Carey v Brown,* 447 U.S. 455, 468 n. 13 (1980).
37. *Runyan v United Brotherhood of Carpenters,* 566 F. Supp. 600 (D. Colo. 1983).
38. 586 F. 2d 530 (5th Cir. 1978), *cert. denied* 444 U.S. 924 (1979).
39. 586 F. 2d at 555, 552. According to one federal district court: "There is a substantial individual interest in the free flow of information regarding abortion." *Valley Family Planning v State of North Dakota,* 489 F. Supp. 238, 242 (D.C.N.D. 1980), *aff'd* 661 F. 2d 99 (8th Cir. 1981).
40. *See Diaz v Oakland Tribune, Inc.,* 139 Cal. App. 3d 118 (1983).
41. 422 U.S. 205 (1975).
42. *Id.* at 210. *See also Chico Feminist Women's Health Center v Butte Glenn Medical Society,* 557 F. Supp. 1190 (E.D. Cal. 1983).

Chapter 12: If You Can Keep It
1. Jacques Ellul, *The Political Illusion* 9 (New York: Vintage Press, 1972).
2. Bertram Gross, *Friendly Fascism: The New Face of Power in America* (New York: M. Evans, 1980).
3. *Id.* at 124.
4. 4 H. A. Washington, ed., *The Writings of Thomas Jefferson* 506 (Philadelphia: J. B. Lippincott, 1869).

Bibliography

Adams, Charles Francis, ed. *The Works of John Adams.* Freeport, New York: Books for Libraries Press, 1969.

"Address to the Inhabitants of Quebec, 1774." I *Journals of the Continental Congress* 1774-1789 (Reprinted by Schwartz, Bernard. *The Bill of Rights: A Documentary History,* Vol. 1. New York: Chelsea House, 1971).

Annals of America, Vol. II. Chicago: Encyclopedia Britannica, Inc., 1968.

Annals of Congress, Vol. III. (1794).

Chafee, Zechariah. *Free Speech in the United States.* Cambridge, Mass.: Harvard University Press, 1941.

Ellul, Jacques. *The Political Illusion.* New York: Vintage Press, 1972

Emerson, Thomas. *The System of Freedom of Expression.* New York: Random House, 1970.

Etelson, Jesse I. "Picketing and Freedom of Speech: Comes the Evolution." 10 *John Marshall Journal of Practice and Procedure* 1 (1976).

Farber, Daniel A. "Commercial Speech and First Amendment Theory." 74 *Northwestern University Law Review* 372 (1979).

Feinberg, Irving Robert. "Picketing, Free Speech and 'Labor Disputes.'" 17 *New York University Law Quarterly* 385 (1940).

Fortas, Abe. *Concerning Dissent and Civil Disobedience.* New York: Signet, 1968.

Frankfurter, Felix and Greene, Nathan. *The Labor Injunction.* Gloucester, Mass.: P. Smith, 1930.

Ginger, Ray. *The Bending Cross: A Biography of Eugene Victor Debs.* New Brunswick, N.J.: Rutgers University Press, 1949.

Gross, Bertram. *Friendly Fascism: The New Face of Power in America.* New York: M. Evans, 1980.

Hall, James Parker. "Free Speech in Wartime." 21 *Columbia Law Review* 527 (1921).

Hawke, David Freeman. *Paine.* New York: Harper and Row, 1974.

Holmes, Oliver Wendell, Jr. "Privilege, Malice and Intent." 8 *Harvard Law Review* 1 (1894).

Hutchinson, William T. and Rachal, William M. E., eds. *The Papers of James Madison* Vol. 1. Chicago: University of Chicago Press, 1962.

Jefferson, Thomas. *The Writings.* S. K. Padover, ed. Lunenberg, Ver.: Stonehour Press, 1967.

Jones, Edgar A., Jr. "The Right to Picket—Twilight Zone of the Constitution." 102 *University of Pennsylvania Law Review* 995 (1954).

Levy, Leonard W. *Legacy of Suppression: Freedom of Speech and Press in Early American History.* Cambridge, Mass.: Belknap Press of Harvard University, 1960.

Lofton, John. *The Press as Guardian of the First Amendment.* Columbia, S.C.: University of South Carolina Press, 1980.

Lyles, J. C. "Skokie as a Symbol." 95 *Christian Century* 412 (1978).

McKay, Robert. "The Preference for Freedom." 34 *New York University Law Review* 1182 (1959).

Meiklejohn, Alexander. *Free Speech and Its Relation to Self-Government* (1948). Port Washington, N.Y.: Kennikat Press, 1972.

Milton, John. "Areopagitica, A Speech for the Liberty of Unlicensed Printing to the Parliament of England" (1644). Reprinted in Norman Dorsen, Paul Bender and Burt Neuborne, eds., *Emerson, Haber, and Dorsen's Political and Civil Rights in the United States,* Vol. 1. Boston, Mass.: Little, Brown, 1976.

Morgan, Howard Wayne. *Eugene V. Debs, Socialist for President.* Syracuse, N.Y.: Syracuse University Press, 1962.

Nelson, Harold L., ed. *Freedom of the Press from Hamilton to the Warren Court.* New York: Bobbs-Merrill Co., 1967.

Nye, Russell Blaine. *Fettered Freedom: Civil Liberties and the Slavery Controversy, 1830 Through 1860.* East Lansing, Mich.: Michigan State University Press, 1964.

Paine, Thomas. *Common Sense; The American Crisis; The Age of Reason.* Franklin Center, Pa.: Franklin Library, 1979.

Redish, Martin H. "The Content Distinction in First Amendment Analysis." 34 *Stanford Law Review* 113 (1981).

Richardson, James D. III. *A Compilation of the Messages and Papers of the Presidents.* New York: Bureau of National Literature, 1897.

"The Right to Receive and Commercial Speech Doctrine: New Constitutional Considerations." Comment, 63 *Georgetown Law Journal* 775 (1975).

Rossiter, Clinton, Joseph Snee, and Arthur E. Sutherland, eds. *Digest of the Public Record of Communism in the United States.* New York: The Fury for the Republic, 1955.

Rutland, Robert Allen. *The Birth of the Bill of Rights.* New York: Collier Books, 1962.

Schlesinger, Arthur M. "Library Trees: A Genealogy." 25 *The New England Quarterly* 435 (December 1952).

Schwartz, Bernard. *The Bill of Rights: A Documentary History.* New York: Chelsea House Publishers, 1971.

Stokes, Anson Phelps. *Church and State in the United States.* New York: Harper and Bros., 1950.

Story, Joseph, III. *Commentaries on the Constitution of the United States.* Boston: Hillard, Gray, and Co., 1833.

"Suspension of the Privilege of the Writ of Habeas Corpus." 10 *Op. Att'y. Gen.* 74 (1861).

Terry, Roderick. "The History of the Liberty Tree of Newport." 27 *Newport Historical Society Bulletin* 9 (1918).

Van Der Weyde, William M., ed. *The Life and Works of Thomas Paine,* Vol. 2. New Rochelle, N.Y.: Thomas Paine National Historical Association, 1925.

Warren, Charles. *Jacobin and Junto.* New York: AMS Press, 1970.

Whipple, Leon. *The Story of Civil Liberties in the United States.* New York: Vanguard Press, 1927.

———. *Our Ancient Liberties.* New York: Da Capo Press, 1970.

Wright, Charles Alan. "The Constitution on the Campus." 22 *Vanderbilt Law Review* 1027 (1969).

Index of Cases

153

Index of Cases

The Author

John W. Whitehead, an attorney specializing in constitutional law, is president of the Rutherford Institute, headquartered near Manassas, Virginia. He has successfully litigated many constitutional law cases.

Mr. Whitehead has taught constitutional law and courses on the First Amendment. He has also lectured at various law schools throughout the United States.

Mr. Whitehead has served as counsel to numerous organizations. He has also served as counsel *amicus curiae* in the United States Supreme Court and various United States Circuit Courts as well as appointed Special Attorney General for the state of Louisiana.

Mr. Whitehead is a member of the bars of the Supreme Courts of Virginia and Arkansas; the United States Supreme Court; the United States Courts of Appeals for the Fourth, Seventh, and Ninth Circuits; and various United States District Courts.

Mr. Whitehead has authored eight books and has coauthored three others. The film version of his book *The Second American Revolution* has been made by Franky Schaeffer V Productions of Los Gatos, California. The movie has been screened in the White House and before congressional staffs in Washington, D.C. It was nationally premiered in November 1982 at the National Archives in Washington, D.C.

Mr. Whitehead has also published articles in both the *Emory Law Journal* and *Texas Tech Law Review* Both concerned First Amendment issues.

He is married and the father of five children.